all Corydoras

*Ulrich Glaser sen.
Frank Schäfer
Wolfgang Glaser*

Verlag: A.C.S. GmbH, Germany

Vorwort
Foreword

AQUALOG ist mit dem Anspruch angetreten, alle Zierfische dieser Erde zu katalogisieren und mit farbigen Abbildungen bestimmbar zu machen. Mit dem nun vorliegenden Band *"all* CORYDORAS" haben wir einen weiteren Schritt auf diesem langen Weg getan.

Wir haben versucht, alle, aber auch wirklich alle Panzerwels-Arten in einem Bildband zusammenzufassen. Besonderes Augenmerk haben wir dabei natürlich auf die besonders beliebte Gattung *Corydoras* gerichtet, aber auch die Gattungen *Aspidoras*, *Brochis*, *Dianema*, *Callichthys* und *Hoplosternum* werden komplett und so umfassend wie noch niemals zuvor dargestellt.

Die drei zuletzt genannten Gattungen werden zur Zeit wissenschaftlich neu bearbeitet. Wir haben zwar teilweise Kenntnis vom derzeitigen Forschungsstand, bevor aber die entsprechenden Arbeiten in der Fachpresse publiziert wurden, haben wir die derzeit gültigen Namen beibehalten.

Einen neuen Weg sind wir bei den bislang nicht eingeführten Arten gegangen: wir haben, so weit vorhanden, die den wissenschaftlichen Erstbeschreibungen beigefügten Zeichnungen übernommen und wo auch diese fehlten, Phantomzeichnungen angefertigt.

Erstmals haben wir in diesem AQUALOG die Arten nicht alphabetisch, sondern nach äußeren Ähnlichkeiten gruppiert. Wir denken, daß es für Sie dadurch noch leichter wird, den von Ihnen gesuchten Fisch zu bestimmen.

Die Liste der gültigen Arten und Teile der Herkunftsangaben haben wir mit freundlicher Genehmigung aus der "Artenliste Panzerwelse" der Herren Rolf Luckow und Hans-Georg Evers übernommen.

Dennoch soll unser Werk selbstverständlich nach wie vor die aquaristische und/oder wissenschaftliche Fachliteratur nicht ersetzen, sondern nur ergänzen.

Das von uns entwickelte Code-Nummern System ermöglicht es, praxisbezogen für Liebhaber und Handel sicherzustellen, daß ein Fisch, unabhängig von seinem aktuellen wissenschaftlichen Status, immer eine stabile Bezeichnung beibehält. Beachten Sie bitte, daß bei uns auch Varianten, Mutanten und Zuchtformen eigene Code-Nummern haben.

Wir wünschen Ihnen viel Freude mit diesem AQUALOG. Sollten Sie Vorschläge haben, wie man künftige AQUALOG-Ausgaben noch besser und anwenderfreundlicher gestalten kann: wir haben immer ein offenes Ohr für Anregungen.

Allen Bildautoren danken wir sehr herzlich für ihre vielfältige Unterstützung.

AQUALOG wants to catalogize and illustrate all known ornamental fish in order to make identificationas as easy as possible. Our newest volume "all CORYDORAS" is another step on this long path that streches in front of us.

We tried very hard to represent all known Plated Catfish species in a single volume. Special references are made on the popular species of *Cory-doras*, but the species of *Aspidoras*, *Brochis*, *Call-ichthys*, *Dianema* and *Hoplosternum* are also de-scribed more careful and detailed than ever before.

The genera *Callichthys*, *Dianema* and *Hoplosternum* are presently under scientific re-examination. Although some of the new material has been available to us, we kept the actual valid names, because so far there has been no official publication on the matter.

Concerning previously unidentified or never imported species, we introduced a new approach: from available original descriptions we give enclosed sketches; in case there were no drawings, photos or paintings at hand, we made up phanthom-sketches ourselves.

For the first time ever AQUALOG uses not an alphabetical order but groups together fish of similar appearance. We are convinced that this will make it even easier for you to identify the fish.

The list of valid names and some of the data on originating are taken of the "Artenliste Panzerwelse" with friendly permission of Rolf Luckow and Hans-Georg Evers.

The purpose of this new reference book is to add to others works on ornamental fish, not to replace them.

Our ingenius Code-number-system enables buyers as well as sellers to steadily identify the fish in question. Please note, that here variations, mutations and breeding-forms have their very own code-number.

We hope you will enjoy AQUALOG. If you should have any comments or suggestions about how to improve this book, we would be glad to hear from you.

We would like to thank all involved photographers for their helpful support.

Mörfelden-Walldorf, April 1996

Ulrich Glaser sen.
Wolfgang Glaser
Frank Schäfer

all CORYDORAS
Was sind Panzerwelse?

Welse gehören zu der riesigen Verwandtschaftsgruppe der Karpfenartigen Fische. Hier bilden die Panzerwelse eine Familie, die Callichthyidae. Zwei Unterfamilien werden unterschieden: die Schwielenwelse, Callichthyinae (Gattungen *Callichthys*, *Hoplosternum* -mit der Untergattung *Cataphractops*- und *Dianema*) und die eigentlichen Panzerwelse, Corydoradinae (Gattungen: *Aspidoras*, *Brochis* und *Corydoras*). Keiner dieser Fische besitzt Schuppen; ihr Körper wird durch große Knochenplatten unter der Schleimhaut wie durch einen Panzer geschützt: daher der Name Panzerwelse. Die Schwielenwelse betreiben alle Brutpflege mit Schaumnestbau, haben ein am Ende des Kopfes liegendes (=endständiges), breiteres Maul, die Panzerwelse hingegen betreiben keine Brutfürsorge und haben ein kleines, an der Unterseite des Kopfes befindliches (=unterständiges) Maul.

Alle Schwielen- und Panzerwelse sind ideale Aquarienfische, mit der einzigen Einschränkung, daß manche Schwielenwelse recht beachtliche Größen erreichen können. Diese hervoragende Eignung kommt in erster Linie daher, daß die Tiere sich auch in der Natur ständig wechselnden Bedingungen anzupassen haben, wozu sie u.a. eine Darmatmung entwickelt haben. Hierbei schlucken die Tiere atmosphärische Luft und entziehen ihr bei der Darmpassage den Sauerstoff. Freilich sollte diese Eigenschaft nicht dazu verführen, die Tiere etwa in dreckigen, ungepflegten Aquarien zu halten. Die Darmatmung ist eine biologische Notlösung, sie dient nicht dem Regelfall. Außerdem kommen manche Panzerwelse, wie z.B. der herrliche *Corydoras barbatus* aus schnellfließenden, kühlen Gewässern. Strapaziert man bei diesen Tieren dauerhaft die Toleranzgrenzen, muß man damit rechnen, daß die Pfleglinge krank werden. In diesem Zusammenhang beachten Sie bitte auch, daß wir bei den Temperaturansprüchen für die einzelnen Arten im beschreibenden Teil immer nur Mittelwerte angeben konnten. Bitte informieren Sie sich in der speziellen Fachliteratur über die individuellen Ansprüche der jeweiligen Arten. Ein, häufig übersehenes, Bedürfnis haben aber alle Panzerwelse: weichen Bodengrund, Besteht der Boden im Aquarium aus Kies oder Lava, so scheuern sich die Tiere zwangsläufig die empfindlichen Barteln ab.

Manche Panzerwels-Arten gelten nach dem Import als empfindlich. Wie schon erwähnt, haben sich die Arten in der Natur mit ständig wechselnden Bedingungen auseinanderzusetzen. Manches mal gehört dazu auch das Austrocknen der Wohngewässer. In Restwassertümpeln finden sich dann u. U. Unmengen von Panzerwelsen. Diese Tiere sind natürlich hochgradig gestresst und vielfältigen Belastungen ausgesetzt. Für die Zierfischsammler in den Ursprungsländern ist diese Notsituation der Fische oft die einzige Möglichkeit, an die Tiere heranzukommen. Zwar werden die gesammelten Exemplare noch vor Ort in Hälterungsanlagen aufgepäppelt; dennoch müssen ihnen, kommen sie schließlich in unsere Aquarien, alle Sorgfalt und Aufmerksamkeit, die möglich ist, entgegengebracht werden, damit sie sich von ihren Strapazen erholen.

Panzerwelse sind auf nahezu dem gesamten Südamerikanischen Subkontinent zu Hause. Manche Arten haben ein riesiges, andere ein kleines Verbreitungsgebiet. Dementsprechend variieren auch die Bedingungen, unter denen die einzelnen Arten zur Fortpflanzung gebracht werden müssen. Dennoch ist bei allen Panzerwelsen, bei denen das bisher ernsthaft versucht wurde, die Fortpflanzung unter Aquarienbedingungen geglückt. Die Geschlechter sind ausnahmslos gut zu unterscheiden, hat man ausgewachsene Tiere vor sich. Dann erscheinen die Weibchen kräftiger und meist auch größer. Betrachtet man die Tiere von oben erkennt man immer, daß bei männlichen Tieren die Brustflossenstacheln verdickt sind. Diese Brustflossenstacheln spielen eine wichtige Rolle bei der Fortpflanzung der Tiere. Das Männchen stellt sich in bestimmten Phasen der Balz T-förmig vor das Weibchen und klemmt die Barteln des Weibchens mit dem Brustflossenstachel fest. Dieses Verhalten scheint bei vielen Arten ein wichtiger Mechanismus zu sein, der unerwünschtes Vermischen (Bastardisieren) der Arten verhindert. Das haben auch die Wissenschaftler erkannt und so ist folgerichtig die Form und Zähnelung des Brustflossenstachels der Männchen ein wichtiges Kriterium bei der Bestimmung nah verwandter Arten.

Allerdings: man sollte nie vergessen, daß solche Mechanismen unter den beengten Bedingungen des Aquariums nicht greifen können. Die gemeinsame Haltung nah verwandter Arten kann daher sehr wohl dazu führen, daß man plötzlich Mischlinge unter seinen Nachzuchten findet.

Wie gesagt, jede Art will etwas unterschiedlich stimuliert werden, möchte man mit ihr züchten. Stammen die Tiere aus Gebieten mit weitgehend konstanten Gegebenheiten, so laichen sie auch im Aquarium oft ganz spontan, ohne daß man großartig etwas getan hätte. Andere reagieren positiv auf Wasserwechsel mit kühlem oder warmem Wasser, wieder andere haben einen Ganz-Jahres-Rhythmus, bei dem die jahreszeitlichen Wechselrhythmen in Bezug auf Licht und Wasserchemie eingehalten werden müssen. Welche Methode bei welcher Art greift, dazu lesen Sie bitte die entsprechenden Publikationen in den Fach-Zeitschriften und -Büchern, der Rahmen unseres, als Bestimmungsbuch ausgelegten Buches, würde bei dem Versuch, alles hierzu bekannte zu referieren, gesprengt.

Abschließend noch etwas zu den Themen "Geselligkeit" und "Fütterung". Wir haben grundsätzlich das Symbol "Schwarmfisch" bei den Corydoras gewählt. Jedoch sind nur bei den Zwerg-Arten, wie z.B. *C. hastatus* und *C. pygmaeus* damit Schwärme von 10-15 Exemplaren gemeint. Die Mehrzahl sollte in Klein-Gruppen von ca. 5 Tieren gepflegt werden. In dieser Gruppenstärke treten viele Arten auch in der Natur auf. Speziell die "Langschnäuzer" legen Wert auf individuellen Freiraum. Und bitte: Panzerwelse sind zwar Allesfresser, jedoch gilt hier wie für alle Fische: wenn Sie züchten möchten (und auch sonst), tun Sie ihren Pfleglingen öfter mal was Gutes in Form von Frost- und Lebendfutter.

all CORYDORAS
How to define Plated Catfish

Among the incredible large group of Cyprinid fish, the Plated Catfish form one distinct family, the Callichthyidae. Two sub-families are defined: the Armoured Catfish, Callichthyinae, and the actual Plated Catfish, the Corydoradinae. None of these fish have any scales; their body is protected by large sheets of bone under the skin: that´s why they are called Plated Catfish. Armoured Catfish are bubble-nest-builders and have a broad mouth at the end of their head. Plated Catfish do not take care of their spawn and have a small mouth at the underside of their head.

All Armoured and Plated Catfish are ideal fish for keeping in tanks; the only abstracle in regard of Armoured Catfish is the respectable size they can grow to. The reason for their unproblematic keeping is due to the fact, that they have developed several strategies in their natural enviroment to adapt to the most different conditions, for example intestinal respiration, which enables them to swallow atmospherical air and gain the oxygene while passing the air through the intestines. This ability should never be an exhause to keep the fish in dirty, neglected tanks. The intestinal respiration is only a biological "emergency exit", it is not meant to work persistantly. Also, some species, like the wonderful Corydoras barbatus, originate from cool, fast running streams; keeping them in bad conditions will definetly cause diseases in a very short time. Keeping this in mind, you should pay attention to the watertemperatures regarding the different species. We can only give you some average data. So please check in any case spezialized literature .on your species to find out the exact needs ofthe fish.

Some Plated Catfish species have been prooved to be extremely sensitive after being imported. The reasons for this are to be found in the circumstances in which the fish are captured. Sometimes the fish have to survive periods of extreme dryness. During this period often an immense number of them have to stay in a very small area of water. This is the only time for native collectors to get hold of the fish. Due to this capturing it is no wonder, the fish very often are extremely stressed when they finally end up in your tank (although every chance to keep the capture and transportation of the fish as stress-free as possible is taken). Still, as soon as you become the new owner of these wonderful fish you should take every necessary step to make them feel as comfortable as possible.

Plated Catfish can be found nearly everywhere on the South American continent. Some species are widely spread, others are not. Therefor breeding conditions differ as much as their occurences. Still, seriously attempted breeding at home always succeeded. The sexes are easily determined as long as you have fully grown fish; females appear bigger and heavier. Looked at from above you can always recognize the thickened pectoral-fin-ray of the male fish. These fin-rays play an important role in the reproduction process: during certain phases of the mating ritual the male fish positions himself T-wise in front of the female and arrests her barbels with his pectoral-fin-ray. This behaviour seems to be an important mechanism to prevent unwanted mingling among different species. Today the form and dentation of the pectoral-fin-ray is a scientifically accepted criteria in distinguishing closely related species. Nevertheless one should never forget that under the cramed conditions in a tank a mingling of different species can definitly happen, so it is always possible to find hybrids among the offspring.

However, every species has its own needs that have to be met in case you want to breed the fish. Do the fish originate from areas with stable living conditions, they often spawn sponanously in captivity. Some react positively to a stimulating change of water temperature, others need to be kept in a full year rhythm with special attention on seasonally changing water chemistry and light. Whatever method you have to apply you will have to look up in a special reference book or scientific magazines, because it is beyond the bounds of this book to give also this kind of information.

Finally, some remarks on social behaviour and feeding procedures: Basically we used the symbol "school fish"for the Corydoras. Still, only the smaller species like Corydoras hastatus, C. pygmaeus etc should be kept in larger groups of 10 - 15 fish. Groups of all other species should not exceed the number of five, because this is the group size a lot of species form in their natural enviroment. Especially the "Long-Noses" enjoy individual areas. And last, but not least: Plated Catfish are definetly omnivorous, but in case you want to succeed in breeding and and keeping (and this is a rule for all fish) you should every now and then treat your pets to a delicious dish of frosted or living food.

Die Schwielenwelse der Unterfamilie Callichthyinae in Umrißzeichnungen
The Plated Catfish of the subfamily Callichthyinae in skeleton paintings

Gattung *Callichthys* SCOPOLI, 1777

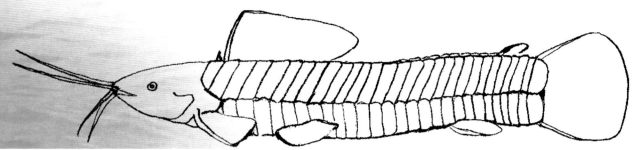

Gattung *Hoplosternum* GILL, 1858

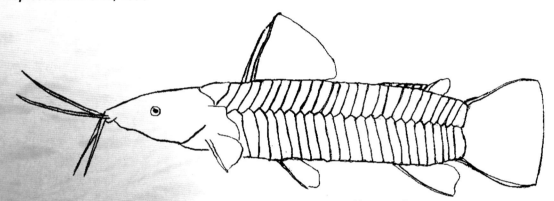

H. pectorale

Untergattung *Cataphractops* FOWLER, 1915

Die einzige bekannte Abbildung von *Hoplosternum* (*Cataphractops*) *melampterus* (COPE, 1871) aus COPE, 1871

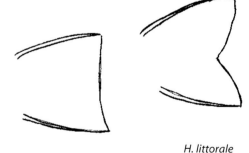

H. thoracatum

H. littorale

Gattung *Dianema* COPE, 1872

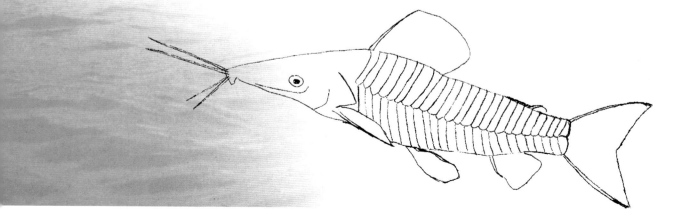

South America **all Corydoras**   © Verlag A.C.S. GmbH

Die Panzerwelse der Unterfamilie Corydoradinae in Umrißzeichnungen
The Plated Catfish of the subfamily Corydoradinae in skeleton paintings

Gattung *Corydoras* LACEPEDE, 1803
Kopfform/*shape of head* "normal"

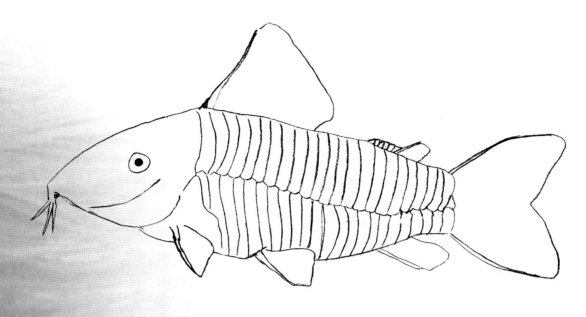

Gattung *Corydoras* LACEPEDE, 1803
Kopfform/*shape of head* "rund/round"

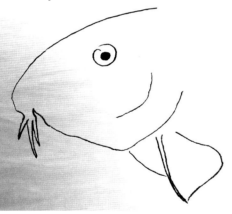

Gattung *Corydoras* LACEPEDE, 1803
Kopfform/*shape of head* "lang/long"

Gattung *Aspidoras* R.v.IHERING, 1907

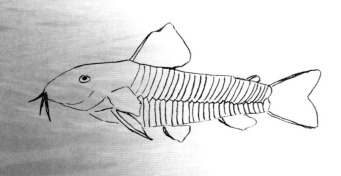

Gattung *Brochis* COPE, 1872

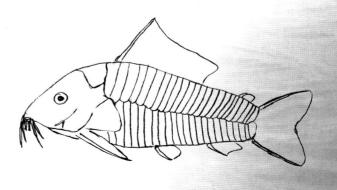

South America **all Corydoras**

Inhalt/*Contents:*

Symbole - Erklärungen *Key to the **symbols***	Innenseite des Deckels *See inside of the cover*
Vorwort/*foreword*	Seite/*page* 3
Einführung/*introduction* Was sind Panzerwelse ? *What are Plated Catfish ?*	Seite 4 *page 5*
Bestimmungsmerkmale der Gattungen *Determination - signs of the genera*	Seiten 6 - 7 *pages 6 - 7*
Schwarz/weiß Zeichnungen bisher nicht eingeführter Arten *Black & white drawings of species not imported yet*	Seiten 9 - 13 *pages 9 - 13*
Liste der gültigen Arten/*list of valid species*	Seiten/*pages* 14 - 15
Bestimmungshilfen/*determination help*	Seite/*page* 16
Bildteil/*plates*	Seiten/*pages* 17 - 122
Lieber Leser/*to our readers*	Seite/*page 123*
Freie Seiten zum Integrieren demnächst erscheinender Ergänzungen *Free pages to stick in the soon coming supplements*	Seiten 124 - 128 *pages*
INDEX Code-numbers	Seiten/*pages 129 - 133*
INDEX alphabet	Seiten/*pages 134 - 138*
INDEX der Bildautoren/*INDEX of the photographers*	Seiten/*pages 139 - 140*
Literatur-Hinweise / Quellenverzeichnis *literature - references / list of sources*	Seiten *141 - 142* *pages*

Erklärungen der Abkürzungen in den wissenschaftlichen Namen
Key to the abbreviations in the scientific names

Normal: *example*   Corydoras bondi coppenamensis
                               Gattung   Art   Unterart
                               Genus   Species   Subspecies

sp.   = die Art ist bislang nicht bestimmt/*the species is not determined yet*
sp. aff. = ähnliche Art/*similar species*
   Erkärung/*explanation*: Es handelt sich um eine bislang unbestimmte Art, die einer bekannten Art jedoch sehr ähnelt/ *a new species, not determined yet, but very similar to a species already known*
cf.   = höchstwahrscheinlich diese Art/*in all probability this species*
   Erkärung/*explanation*: Die vorliegenden Exemplare weichen in gewissen Details von der Originalbeschreibung ab, jedoch nicht so gravierend, daß es sich dabei mit einiger Wahrscheinlichkeit um eine andere Art handelt/ *the specimen examined differs in some details from the original description, but not so grave, that it seems (with some probability) to be a different species*
ssp.   = Unterart/*subspecies*
   Erkärung/*explanation*:Einige Arten haben ein sehr großes Verbreitungsgebiet; innerhalb dieses Gebietes gibt es Populationen, die sich äußerlich zwar deutlich von anderen Populationen unterscheiden, genetisch jedoch zur gleichen Art gehören. Solchen Populationen erhalten als geografische Unterart einen dritten wissenschaftlichen Namen. Ist die Unterart bislang unbestimmt, so steht hier nur ssp../*Some species inhabit an area of very wide range; within this area there are populations that differ optical significant from other populations, seen in genetic case, they own nevertheless to the same species. Those populations get a third scientific name as geographical subspecies. Is the subspecies not determined yet, on this place only stands ssp..*
var.   = Variante/*variation*
   Erkärung/*explanation*: Individuelle Abweichungen in der Farbe, die nicht geografisch fixiert werden können, werden als Varianten bezeichnet. Sie erhalten keine eigene wissenschaftliche Bezeichnung./ *Individual differences in coloration, which are not fixed in geografical areas, are so-called variations. They don´t get a special scientific name.*
Hybride   : Mischling zwischen zwei Arten/*crossbreed between two species*
intergrade: gemischte Population zwischen zwei Unterarten/*mixed population between two subspecies*

Bisher nicht oder nur einmal eingeführte Arten
species not (or only once) imported yet

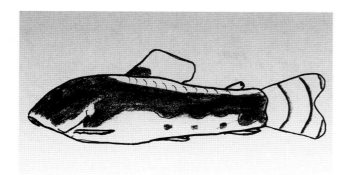

S06105 *Aspidoras brunneus* (sketch by F. Schäfer)
2,5 - 3,5 cm
Brasilien: Est Mato Grosso, Serra do Roncador

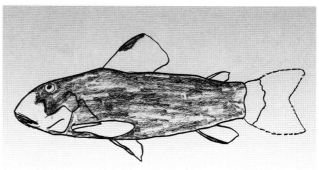

S06108 *Aspidoras carvalhoi* (sketch by F. Schäfer)
3,5 - 4 cm
Brasilien: Est. Ceara, Acude Canabrara, Rio de Janeiro

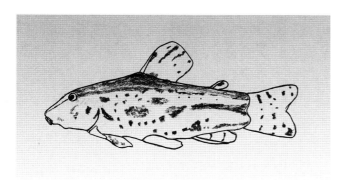

S06112 *Aspidoras fuscoguttatus* (sketch by F. Schäfer)
4 - 4,5 cm
Brasilien: Est. Mato Grosso, Rio Parana-System, Corrego Corguinho

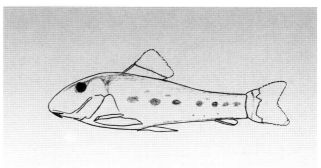

S06118 *Aspidoras maculosus* (sketch by F. Schäfer)
4 - 4,5 cm
Brasilien: Est. Bahia, Rio Paiaia, Rio Agua Branca, Rio Zinga

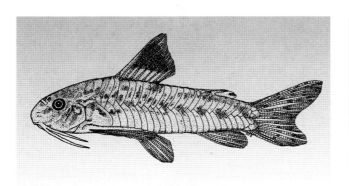

S06130 *Aspidoras raimundi* (taken from NIJSSEN & ISBRÜCKER, 1976)
male, 3,5 - 4 cm
Brasilien: Est. Maranhao, Rio Parnahyba-System

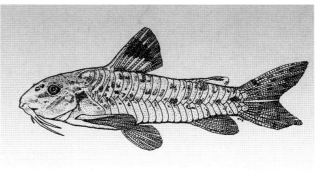

S06130 *Aspidoras raimundi* (taken from NIJSSEN & ISBRÜCKER, 1976)
female, 3,5 - 4 cm
Brasilien: Est. Maranhao, Rio Parnahyba-System

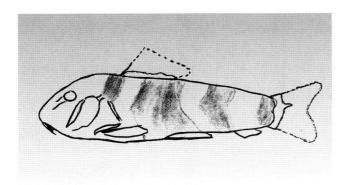

S06135 *Aspidoras rochai* (sketch by F. Schäfer)
4 cm
Brasilien: Est. Ceara, Fortaleza

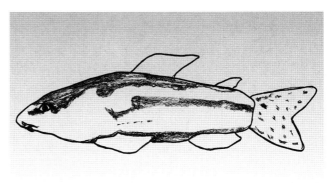

S06165 *Aspidoras virgulatus* (sketch by F. Schäfer)
4 - 4,5 cm
Brasilien: Est. Espirito Santo, Seitenarme/branches des Rio Doce

Bisher nicht oder nur einmal eingeführte Arten
species not (or only once) imported yet

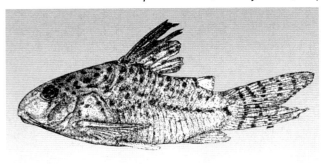

S18010 *Corydoras acrensis* (taken from NIJSSEN, 1972)
3,5 - 4 cm
Brasilien: Est. Acre, Furo do Lago Sao Francisco

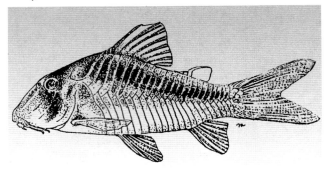

S18265 *Corydoras amapaensis* (taken from NIJSSEN, 1972)
6,5 - 7 cm   Brasilien: Est. Amapa, Cachoera Creek, Aqua Branca Creek. French Guyana: Maroni-River Syst., Rio Oyapock System.

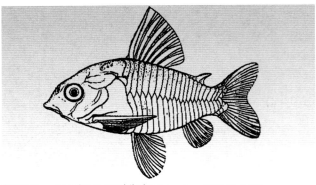

S18300 *Corydoras amphibelus* (taken from FOWLER, 1941)
3,5 - 4 cm
Peru: Edo. Loreto, Rio Ampiyacu bei/near Pebas

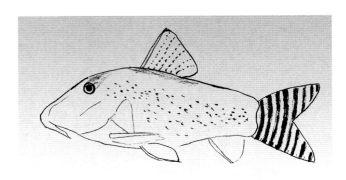

S18310 *Corydoras approuaguensis* (sketch by F. Schäfer)
5,5 - 6 cm
French Guiana: Approuague River

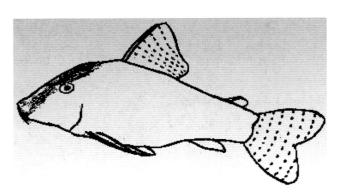

S18425 *Corydoras aurofrenatus* (Phantom-sketch by F. Schäfer)
6 - 6,5 cm
Paraguay: Aguada near Arroyo Trementina, Villa Rica

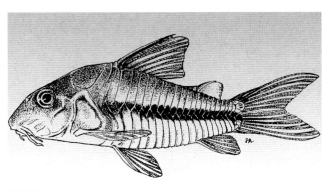

S18515 *Corydoras baderi* (taken from NIJSSEN, 1970)
5,5 - 6 cm
Brasilien: Est. Par, Rio Paru de Oeste; Surinam: Morowinje River Syst.

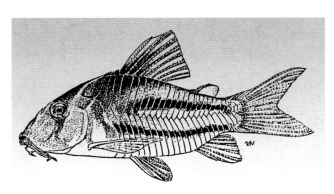

S18576 *Corydoras bifasciatus* (taken from NIJSSEN, 1972)
5,5 - 6 cm
Surinam: Corantijn System, Sipaliwini River, Lucie River

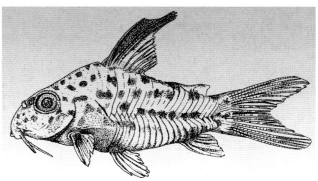

S18530 *Corydoras boehlkei* (taken from NIJSSEN & ISBRÜCKER, 1982)
3 - 3,5 cm
Venezuela: Edo Bolivar, Rio Cuchime

Bisher nicht oder nur einmal eingeführte Arten
species not (or only once) imported yet

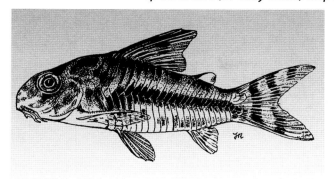

S18540 *Corydoras boesemani* (taken from NIJSSEN & ISBRÜCKER, 1982)
4,5 - 5 cm
Surinam: Brokopondo Distrikt

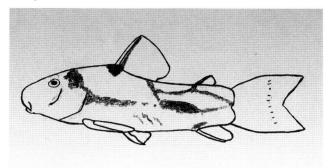

S18630 *Corydoras carlae* (sketch by F. Schäfer)
4,5 - 5 cm
Argentinien: Provinz Misiones, Parana-Becken

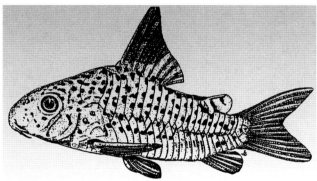

S18860 *Corydoras copei* (taken from NIJSSEN & ISBRÜCKER, 1986)
4,5 - 5 cm
French Guyana: Rio Oyapock-System

S18860 *Corydoras ephippifer* (taken from NIJSSEN, 1972)
5,5 - 6 cm
Paraguay: Sapucay, Arroyo Pona

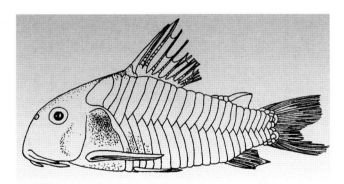

S18885 *Corydoras esperanzae* (taken from CASTRO, 1987)
5,5 - 6 cm
Brasilien: Rio Amazonas bei Codajas

S18920 *Corydoras filamentosus* (sketch by F. Schäfer)
3,5 - 4 cm
Brasilien: oberer Rio Solimoes

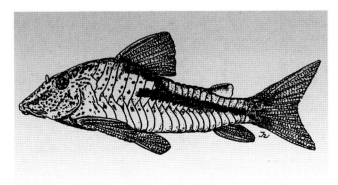

S18935 *Corydoras fowleri* (taken from NIJSSEN & ISBRÜCKER, 1986)
7 - 7,5 cm
Brasilien: Rio Piracica Sytem near Sao Paulo

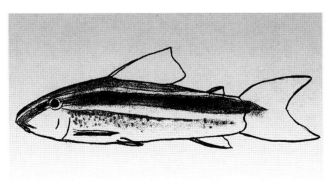

S18995 *Corydoras gracilis* (sketch by F. Schäfer)
3,5 - 4 cm
Brasilien: Est. Rondonia, Rio Marmore-System

Bisher nicht oder nur einmal eingeführte Arten
species not (or only once) imported yet

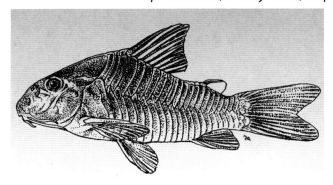

S19015 *Corydoras guianensis* (taken from NIJSSEN 1970)
5,5 - 6 cm
Brasilien: Est. Rondonia, Rio Guapore

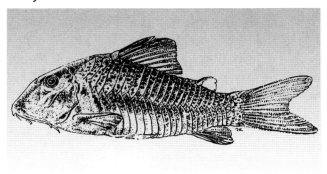

S19045 *Corydoras heteromorphus* (taken from NIJSSEN 1970)
6,5 - 7 cm
Brasilien: Est. Amazonas, Villa Bella, Est. Mato Grosso, Pantanal

S19110 *Corydoras lamberti* (taken from NIJSSEN & ISBRÜCKER, 1986)
4,5 - 5 cm
Brasilien: Bahia, RioRibeira da Terra Firme, Rio Ribeira Grande

S19360 *Corydoras micracanthus* (phantom-sketch by F. Schäfer)
5,5 - 6 cm
Kolumbien: Rio Meta, Barrigon

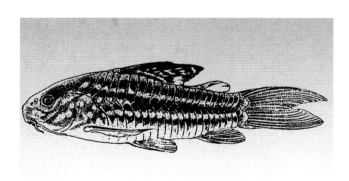

S19385 *Corydoras nanus* (taken from NIJSSEN 1970)
5 - 5,5 cm
Brasilien: Rio Sao Francisco, upper Rio Solimoes

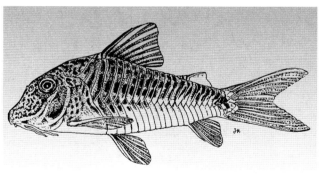

S19500 *Corydoras octocirrhus* (taken from NIJSSEN 1970)
7 - 7,5 cm
Brasilien: Rio Parnahyba, Rio de Janeiro, Rio Juquia, Poco Grande

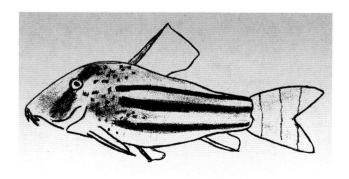

S19531 *Corydoras ornatus* (sketch by F. Schäfer)
6,5 - 7 cm
Französisch Guyana: Cumuri Creek, Campori River

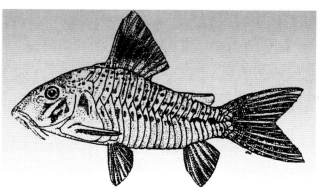

S19545 *Corydoras orphnopterus* (taken from WEITZMAN & NIJSSEN, 1970)
6,5 - 7 cm
Brasilien: Est. Para, Rio Tapajosi

Bisher nicht oder nur einmal eingeführte Arten
species not (or only once) imported yet

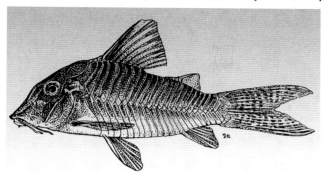

S19575 Corydoras oxyrhynchus (taken from NIJSSEN, 1970)
5,5 - 6 cm
Brasilien: Est. Acre, Rio Iquir

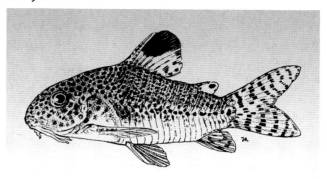

S19735 *Corydoras punctatus* (taken from NIJSSEN, 1970)
5,5 - 6 cm
Guyana - Länder

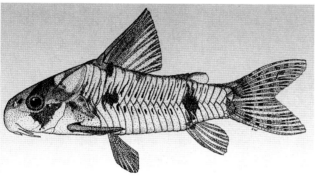

S19800 *Corydoras reynoldsi* (taken from MYERS & WEITZMAN, 1960)
3,5 - 4 cm
Argentinien: Provinz Jujuy, Sunchal

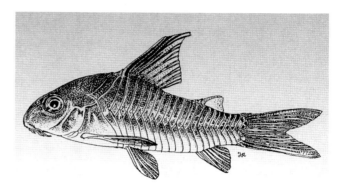

S19830 *Corydoras sanchesi* (taken from NIJSSEN, 1970)
4,5 - 5 cm
Brasilien: Est. Amazonas, Rio Purus System

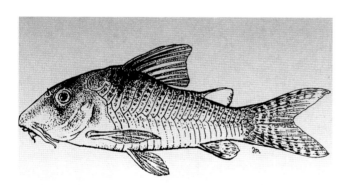

S19841 *Corydoras saramaccensis* (taken from NIJSSEN, 1970)
5,5 - 6 cm
Surinam: Saramacca-System, Gojo Creek

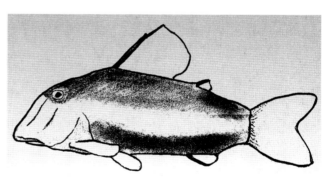

S20700 *Corydoras spilurus* (sketch by F. Schäfer)
5,5 - 6 cm
Brasilien: Est. Amapa, Rio Oyapock

S20970 *Corydoras weitzmani* (taken from NIJSSEN, 1971)
5,5 - 6 cm
Peru: Est. Cuzco bei/near Cusco

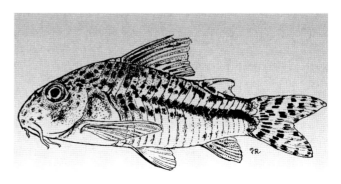

S18568 Naturhybride / Nature-Hybrid zwischen / between
Corydoras bondi coppenamensis und *Corydoras surinamensis*
(taken from NIJSSEN, 1970). Surinam: Coppenam River

South America **all Corydoras**

Liste der gültigen Arten der Familie Callichthyidae
list of the valid species of the familiy Callichthyidae

Aspidoras	R. v. IHERING, 1907
A. albater	Nijssen & Isbrücker, 1976
A. brunneus	Nijssen & Isbrücker, 1976
A. carvalhoi	Nijssen & Isbrücker, 1976
A. eurycephalus	Nijssen & Isbrücker, 1976
A. fuscoguttatus	Nijssen & Isbrücker, 1976
A. lakoi	Miranda-Ribeiro, 1949
A. maculosus	Nijssen & Isbrücker, 1976
A. menezesi	Nijssen & Isbrücker, 1976
A. pauciradiatus	(Weitzman & Nijssen, 1970)
A. poecilus	Nijssen & Isbrücker, 1976
A. raimundi	(Steindachner, 1907)
A. rochai	v. Ihering, 1907
A. spilotus	Nijssen & Isbrücker, 1976
A. virgulatus	Nijssen & Isbrücker, 1980
Brochis	COPE, 1872
B. britskii	Nijssen & Isbrücker, 1983
B. multiradiatus	(Orces-Villagomez, 1960)
B. splendens	(Castelnau, 1855)
Corydoras	LACÉPÈDE, 1803
C. acrensis	Nijssen, 1972
C. acutus	Cope, 1872
C. adolfoi	Burgess, 1982
C. aeneus	(Gill, 1858)
C. agassizii	Steindachner, 1877
C. amandajanea	Sands, 1995
C. amapaensis	Nijssen, 1972
C. ambiacus	Cope, 1872
C. amphibelus	Cope, 1872
C. approuaguensis	Nijssen & Isbrücker, 1993
C. araguaiaensis	Sands, 1990
C. arcuatus (=C20)	Elwin, 1939
C. armatus	(Günther, 1868)
C. atropersonatus	Weitzman & Nijssen, 1970
C. aurofrenatus	Eigenmann & Kennedy, 1903
C. australis	(Eigenmann & Ward, 1907)
C. axelrodi	Rössel, 1962
C. baderi	Geisler, 1969
C. barbatus	(Quoy & Gaimard, 1824)
C. bicolor	Nijssen & Isbrücker, 1967
C. bifasciatus	Nijssen, 1972
C. blochi blochi	Nijssen, 1971
C. blochi vittatus	Nijssen, 1971
C. boehlkei	Nijssen & Isbrücker, 1982
C. boesemani	Nijssen & Isbrücker, 1967
C. bolivianus	Nijssen & Isbrücker, 1983
C. bondi bondi	Gosline, 1940
C. bondi coppenamensis	Nijssen, 1970
C. breei	Nijssen & Isbrücker, 1992
C. burgessi	Axelrod, 1987
C. carlae	Nijssen & Isbrücker, 1983
C. caudimaculatus	Rössel, 1961
C. cervinus	Rössel, 1962
C. cochui	Myers & Weitzmann, 1954
C. concolor	Weitzmann, 1961
C. condiscipulus	Nijssen & Isbrücker, 1980
C. copei	Nijssen & Isbrücker, 1986
C. cortesi	Castro, 1987
C. crypticus	Sands, 1995
C. davidsandsi	Black, 1988
C. delphax	Nijssen & Isbrücker, 1983
C. duplicareus	Sands, 1995
C. ehrhardti	Steindachner, 1910
C. elegans	Steindachner, 1877
C. ellisae	Gosline, 1940
C. ephippifer	Nijssen, 1972
C. eques	Steindachner, 1877
C. esperanzae	Castro, 1987
C. evelynae	Rössel, 1963
C. filamentosus	Nijssen & Isbrücker, 1983
C. flaveolus	R.v.Ihering, 1911
C. fowleri	Boehlke, 1950
C. garbei	R.v.Ihering, 1911
C. geryi	Nijssen & Isbrücker, 1983
C. gomezi	Castro, 1986
C. gossei	Nijssen, 1972
C. gracilis	Nijssen & Isbrücker, 1976
C. griseus	Holly, 1940
C. guapore	Knaak, 1961
C. guianensis	Nijssen, 1970
C. habrosus	Weitzman, 1960
C. haraldschultzi	Knaak, 1961
C. hastatus	Eigenmann & Eigenmann, 1888
C. heteromorphus	Nijssen, 1970
C. imitator	Nijssen & Isbrücker, 1983
C. incolicana (=C1)	Burgess, 1993
C. julii	Steindachner, 1906
C. lacerdai (=C15)	Hieronimus, 1995
C. lamberti	Nijssen & Isbrücker, 1986
C. latus	Pearson, 1924
C. leopardus	Myers, 1933
C. leucomelas	Eigenmann & Allen, 1942
C. loretoensis	Nijssen & Isbrücker, 1986
C. loxozonus	Nijssen & Isbrücker, 1983
C. macropterus	Regan, 1913
C. maculifer	Nijssen & Isbrücker, 1971
C. melanistius melanistius	Regan, 1912
C. melanistius brevirostris	Fraser-Brunner, 1947
C. melanotaenia	Regan, 1912
C. melini	Lönnberg & Rendahl, 1930
C. metae	Eigenmann, 1914
C. micracanthus?	Regan, 1912
C. multimaculatus	Steindachner, 1907
C. nanus	Nijssen & Isbrücker, 1967
C. napoensis	Nijssen & Isbrücker, 1986
C. narcissus	Nijssen & Isbrücker, 1980
C. nattereri	Steindachner, 1877
C. >nijsseni<	Sands, 1990
C. octocirrus	Nijssen, 1970
C. oiapoquensis	Nijssen, 1972
C. ornatus	Nijssen & Isbrücker, 1976
C. orphnopterus	Weitzman & Nijssen, 1970
C. osteocarus	Böhlke, 1951
C. ourastigma	Nijssen, 1972
C. oxyrhynchus	Nijssen & Isbrücker, 1967
C. paleatus	(Jenyns, 1842)

Liste der gültigen Arten der Familie Callichthyidae
list of the valid species of the familiy Callichthyidae
Forts./continue

C. panda	Nijssen & Isbrücker, 1971	
C. parallelus (=C2)	Burgess, 1993	
C. pastazensis	Weitzman, 1963	
C. pinheiroi (=C25)	Dinkelmeyer, 1995	
C. polystictus	Regan, 1912	
C. potaroensis	Myers, 1927	
C. prionotus	Nijssen & Isbrücker, 1980	
C. pulcher	Nijssen & Isbrücker, 1980	
C. punctatus	(Bloch, 1794)	
C. pygmaeus	Knaak, 1966	
C. rabauti	LaMonte, 1941	
C. reticulatus	Fraser-Brunner, 1938	
C. revelatus	Cockerell, 1923	
C. reynoldsi	Myers & Weitzman, 1960	
C. robinae	Burgess, 1983	
C. robustus	Nijssen & Isbrücker, 1980	
C. sanchesi	Nijssen & Isbrücker, 1967	
C. saramaccensis	Nijssen, 1970	
C. sarareensis (=C23)	Dinkelmeyer, 1995	
C. schwartzi	Rössel, 1963	
C. semiaquilus	Weitzman, 1964	
C. septentrionalis	Gosline, 1940	
C. serratus	Sands, 1995	
C. seussi (=C27)	Dinkelmeyer, 1996	
C. similis	Hieronimus, 1991	
C. simulatus	Weitzman & Nijssen, 1970	
C. sodalis	Nijssen & Isbrücker, 1986	
C. solox	Nijssen & Isbrücker, 1983	
C. spilurus	Norman, 1926	
C. steindachneri	Isbrücker & Nijssen, 1973	
C. stenocephalus	Eigenmann & Allen, 1942	
C. sterbai	Knaak, 1962	
C. surinamensis	Nijssen, 1970	
C. sychri	Weitzman, 1960	
C. treitlii	Steindachner, 1906	
C. trilineatus	Cope, 1872	
C. undulatus	Regan, 1912	
C. virginiae (=C4)	Burgess, 1993	
C. weitzmani	Nijssen, 1971	
C. xinguensis	Nijssen, 1972	
C. zygatus	Eigenmann & Allen, 1942	
Callichthys	SCOPOLI, 1777	
C. callichthys	(Linnaeus, 1758)	
Dianema	COPE, 1872	
D. longibarbis	Cope, 1872	
D. urostriata	Miranda Ribeiro, 1912	
Hoplosternum	GILL, 1858	
H. littorale	(Hancock, 1828)	
H. pectorale	(Boulenger, 1825)	
H. thoracatum	(Valanciennes, 1840)	

C - Welse

C 1	= *Corydoras incoliana* Burgess, 1993
C 2	= *Corydoras parallelus* Burgess, 1993
C 3	= similar *Corydoras sychri*
C 4	= *Corydoras virginae* Burgess, 1993
C 5	= similar *Corydoras latus*
C 6	= similar *Corydoras surinamensis*
C 7	= similar *Corydoras macropterus*
C 8	= similar *Corydoras habrosus*
C 9	= similar *Corydoras leopardus*
C 10	= similar *Corydoras melanistius* und *Corydoras leucomelas*
C 11	= body like *Corydoras guapore*, colour like *Corydoras julii*
C 12	= similar *Corydoras lamberti*
C 13	= similar *Corydoras evelynae*
C 14	= similar *Corydoras polystictus*
C 15	= *Corydoras lacerdai* Hieronimus, 1995
C 16	= similar *Corydoras melini*
C 17	= similar *Corydoras ellisae*
C 18	= similar *Corydoras orphnopterus*
C 19	= similar *Corydoras evelynae*
C 20	= similar *Corydoras arcuatus*
C 21	= similar *Corydoras melanistius*
C 22	= similar *Corydoras paleatus*
C 23	= *Corydoras sarareensis* Dinkelmeyer, 1995
C 24	= similar *Corydoras blochi*
C 25	= *Corydoras pinheiroi* Dinkelmeyer, 1995
C 26	= similar *Corydoras atropersonatus*
C 27	= *Corydoras seussi* Dinkelmeyer, 1995
C 28	= similar *Corydoras blochi*
C 29	= similar *Corydoras cervinus*
C 30	= similar *Corydoras bicolor*
C 31	= similar *Corydoras bondi*
C 32	= similar *Corydoras blochi*
C 33	= similar *Corydoras atropersonatus*
C 34	= similar *Corydoras melanistius*
C 35	= *Aspidoras* sp. "Black Phantom"
C 36	= *Aspidoras* sp. "Araguaia"
C 37	= *Aspidoras* sp. "Goia"
C 38	= similar *Corydoras serratus*
C 39	= similar *Corydoras imitator*
C 40	= similar *C.orydoras griseus*
C 41	= similar *Corydoras napoensis*
C 42	= similar *Corydoras blochi*
C 43	= similar *Corydoras ambiacus*
C 44	= similar *Corydoras surinamensis*
C 45	= similar *Corydoras araguaiensis*
C 46	= similar *Corydoras atropersonatus*

Who is who bei Corydoras

Bitte beachten Sie: das unten angegebene Raster ist nur sehr grob
Please remark: the scheme given here is only crude

S./pp. 20-46
- schwarze Augenbinde
- *black eye-band*
- Körper +/- punktiert
- *body +/- spotted*

S./pp. 46-63
- keine schwarze Augenbinde
- *black eye-band absent*
- Körper +/- punktiert
- *body +/- spotted*

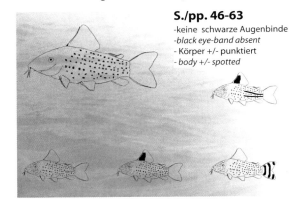

S./pp. 63-79
- Körper auffällig schwarz/weiß gezeichnet
- *body striking black & white*

S./pp. 80-92
- Körper +/- unregelmäßig gebändert und gefleckt
- *body more or less irregular banded and mottled*

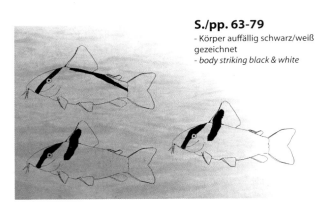
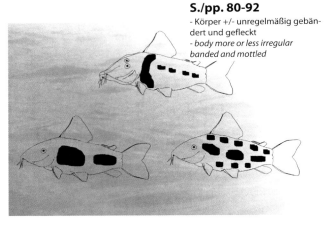

S./pp. 93-94
- schwarze Mittelbinde
- *black middle-band*

S./pp. 95-96
- schwarze Augenbinde
- *black eye-band*
- zwei schwarze körperbinden
- *two black body-bands*

S./pp. 96-97
- Körperbinde kann in Einzelflecken aufgelöst sein
- *body-band may be untidy into spots*

S./pp. 97-100
- Körper-Hauptfarbe schwarz Fische sehr langgestreckt
- *main body-colour black, very elongate fishes*

S./pp. 101-104
- zwischen drei dunklen Bändern helle Glanzstreifen
- *between three dark bands bright stripes*

S./pp. 104-111
- metallischer Glanz auf dem ganz Körper
- *hole body metalic shinig*

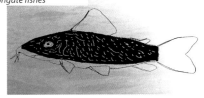
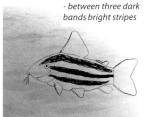

S./pp. 111-113
- schwarze Rückenbinde
- *black band on the back*

S./pp. 113-116
- Körper-Hauptfarbe schwarz Fische sehr hochrückig
- *main body-colour black, very high-bodied fishes*

S./pp. 116-117
- großer schwarzer Caudalfleck
- *black large caudal-spot*

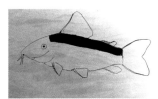
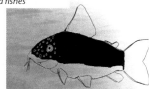

South America all Corydoras © Verlag A.C.S. GmbH

S06102-3 Aspidoras albater
W, 3,5 - 4cm
Brazil: Est. Goias, RioTocantinzinha by Sao Joao da Alianca.

S06102-3 Aspidoras albater
W, 3,5 - 4cm
Brazil: Est. Goias, RioTocantinzinha by Sao Joao da Alianca.

S06110-3 Aspidoras cf. eurycephalus
W, 2,5 - 3,5cm
Brazil: Est. Goias, Rio Tocantins-System; Rio das Almas/Maranhao

S06110-3 Aspidoras cf. eurycephalus
W, 2,5 - 3,5cm
Brazil: Est. Goias, Rio Tocantins-System; Rio das Almas/Maranhao

S05115-3 Aspidoras lakoi
W, 3,5 - 4cm
Brazil: Est. Minas Gerais, Rio Parana-System, branch of Rio-Grande

S05115-3 Aspidoras lakoi
W, 3,5 - 4cm
Brazil: Est. Minas Gerais, Rio Parana-System, branch of Rio-Grande

S06119-3 Aspidoras cf. maculosus
Synonym: A.rochai ELLIS, 1913 W, 3,5 - 4,5cm
Brazil: Est. Bahia, Rio Paiaia, Rio Aqua Branca, Rio Zinga

S06119-3 Aspidoras cf. maculosus
Synonym: A.rochai ELLIS, 1913 W, 3,5 - 4,5cm
Brazil: Est. Bahia, Rio Paiaia, Rio Aqua Branca, Rio Zinga

South America **all Corydoras**

S06121-3 Aspidoras menezesi MALE
W, 4- 5cm
Brazil: Est. Ceara, Rio Granjeiro by Crato, Rio Salgado-System

S06121-3 Aspidoras menezesi FEMALE
W, 4- 5cm
Brazil: Est. Ceara, Rio Granjeiro by Crato, Rio Salgado-System

S06121-3 Aspidoras menezesi MALE
W, 4- 5cm
Brazil: Est. Ceara, Rio Granjeiro by Crato, Rio Salgado-System

S06123-3 Aspidoras pauciradiatus MALE, W, 2,5 - 3cm
Syn.: C.pauciradiatus WEITZM.+NIJSSEN, 1970; C.U6 AXELROD,1967
Brazil: Est. Goias, Rio Araguaia by Aruna; Est. Amazonas, Rio Negro.

S06123-3 Aspidoras pauciradiatus FEMALE, W, 2,5 - 3cm
Syn.:C. pauciradiatus; Weitzmann+Nijssen,1970; C.P-6 Axelrod 1967
Brazil: Est. Goias, Rio Araguaia by Aruna; Est. Amazonas, Rio Negro.

S06126-3 Aspidoras cf. poecilus MALE, W, 3,5 - 4cm
Synonym: Corydoras cochui(Axelrod 1967); C.rochai(Knaack 1970)
Brazil: Est. Mato Grosso, Rio Xingu; Est. Goias, Rio Araguaia.

S06140-3 Aspidoras sp. "ARAGUAIA" (C 36) MALE
W, 3 - 4cm
Brazil: Est. Goias, Rio Araguaia - area.

S06145-3 Aspidoras sp. "BLACK - PHANTOM" (C 35) PAIR
W, 3,5 - 4,5cm
Brazil: Est. Goias, Rio Araguaia - area.

S06145-3 Aspidoras sp. "BLACK - PHANTOM" (C 35) MALE
W, 3,5 - 4,5cm
Brazil: Est. Goias, Rio Araguaia - area.

S06145-3 Aspidoras sp. "BLACK - PHANTOM" (C 35) FEMALE
W, 3,5 - 4,5cm
Brazil: Est. Goias, Rio Araguaia - area.

S06150-3 Aspidoras sp. "GOIA" (C 37) MALE
W, 3 - 4cm
Brazil: Est. Goias, Rio Tesouras (tributary of Rio Peixe).

S09105-4 Brochis britskii
W, 10 - 12cm
Brazil: Est. Mato Grosso, Rio-Paraguay-system by Pocone + Miranda

S09105-4 Brochis britskii
W, 10 - 12cm
Brazil: Est. Mato Grosso, Rio-Paraguay-system by Pocone + Mirinda

S09110-4 Brochis multiradiatus   W, 9 - 10cm
Synonym: Chaenothorax multiradiatus ORCES-VILLAGOMEZ, 1960
Brazil: Rio Madeira-area; Peru: Rio Ucayali+Nanay; Ecuador: Lagarto

S09110-4 Brochis multiradiatus   W, 9 - 10cm
Synonym: Chaenothorax multiradiatus ORCES-VILLAGOMEZ, 1960
Brazil: Rio Madeira-area; Peru: Rio Ucayali+Nanay; Ecuador: Lagarto

S09110-4 Brochis multiradiatus   W, 9 - 10cm
Synonym: Chaenothorax multiradiatus ORCES-VILLAGOMEZ, 1960
Brazil: Rio Madeira-area; Peru: Rio Ucayali+Nanay; Ecuador: Lagarto

S09120-4 Brochis splendens   adult
Synonym: Lichthys splendens; C.taiposh; Hoplosoma splendens;
C.semisculatus; Chenothorax bicarinatus, W, 7-8cm,Brazil+Peru+Ec

S09120-2 Brochis splendens   semiadult
Synonym: Lichthys splendens; C.taiposh; Hoplosoma splendens;
C.semisculatus; Chenothorax bicarinatus, W, 7-8cm,Brazil+Peru+Ec

S09123-3 Brochis splendens   "SPOTTED"
Synonym: Lichthys splendens; C.taiposh; Hoplosoma splendens;
C.semisculatus; Chenothorax bicarinatus, W, 7-8cm,Brazil+Peru+Ec

S09125 Brochis splendens   "BLACK"
Synonym: Lichthys splendens; C.taiposh; Hoplosoma splendens;
C.semisculatus; Chenothorax bicarinatus, W, 7-8cm,Brazil+Peru+Ec

S09125-4 Brochis splendens   "BLACK"
Synonym: Lichthys splendens; C.taiposh; Hoplosoma splendens;
C.semisculatus; Chenothorax bicarinatus, W, 7-8cm,Brazil+Peru+Ec

S18015-2 Corydoras acutus   semiadult
    W, 6 - 7cm
Ecuador: Rio Napo-system; Peru: Rio Ampiyacu + Rio Yavari.

S18015-4 Corydoras acutus   MALE
    W, 6 - 7cm
Ecuador: Rio Napo-system; Peru: Rio Ampiyacu + Rio Yavari.

S18015-4 Corydoras acutus   adult
    W, 6 - 7cm
Ecuador: Rio Napo-system; Peru: Rio Ampiyacu + Rio Yavari.

S18605-4 CORYDORAS BLOCHI VITTATUS "VARIANTE"

S18405-4 Corydoras atropersonatus
W, 4 - 5cm
Ecuador: Est. Pastaza, Rio Tigre-system+Shione; Peru: Rio Nanayi

S18405-4 Corydoras atropersonatus
W, 4 - 5cm
Ecuador: Est. Pastaza, Rio Tigre-system+Shione; Peru: Rio Nanayi

S18415-4 Corydoras atropersonatus "VARIANTE I"
W, 4 - 5cm
Ecuador: Est. Pastaza, Rio Tigre-system+Shione; Peru: Rio Nanayi

S18418-4 Corydoras atropersonatus "VARIANTE II"
W, 4 - 5cm
Ecuador: Est. Pastaza, Rio Tigre-system+Shione; Peru: Rio Nanayi

S18419-2 Corydoras atropersonatus "VARIANTE III" semiadult
W, 4 - 5cm
Ecuador: Est. Pastaza, Rio Tigre-system+Shione; Peru: Rio Nanayi

S18595-4 Corydoras cf. blochi blochi
W, 5 - 6cm
Brazil: Est.Roaima, Rio Branco-syst.;Amazonas; Guyana + Venezuela

S18595-4 Corydoras cf. blochi blochi "INTERRUPT - BAND"
W, 5 - 6cm
Brazil: Est.Roaima, Rio Branco-syst.;Amazonas; Guyana +Venezuela

S18590-4 Corydoras cf. blochi blochi
W, 5 - 6cm
Brazil: Est.Roaima, Rio Branco-syst.;Amazonas; Guyana +Venezuela

South America **all Corydoras**

S18585-4 Corydoras sp. aff. blochi blochi
 W, 5 - 6cm
Brazil: Est.Roaima, Rio Branco-syst.;Amazonas; Guyana +Venezuela

S18600-2 Corydoras blochi vittatus   JUVENIL
 W, 5 - 6cm
Brazil: Est. Maranhao, branch of Rio Hapecuru by Caxias.

S18600-4 Corydoras blochi vittatus   ADULT
 W, 5 - 6cm
Brazil: Est. Maranhao, branch of Rio Hapecuru by Caxias.

S18600-4 Corydoras blochi vittatus
 W, 5 - 6cm
Brazil: Est. Maranhao, branch of Rio Hapecuru by Caxias.

S18515-4 Corydoras sp. aff. blochi vittatus
 W, 5 - 6cm
Brazil: Est. Maranhao, branch of Rio Hapecuru by Caxias.

S18900-4 Corydoras evelynae echter/true one!
 W, 4 - 5cm
Columbia: Rio Meta, Cano Orocue by Orocue.

S18903-4 Corydoras evelynae "VARIANTE"
 W, 4 - 5cm
 Columbia: Rio Meta.

S18906-4 Corydoras evelynae "VARIANTE I" square-spotted!
 W, 4 - 5cm
 Columbia: Rio Meta.

South America **all Corydoras**

S19260-4 CORYDORAS MELANISTIUS BREVIROSTRIS PAIR

S19650-2 CORYDORAS PARALLELUS "C 02" semiadult

S18906-4 Corydoras evelynae "VARIANTE I"
W, 4 - 5cm
Columbia: Rio Meta.

S19840-4 Corydoras cf. saramaccensis
W, 5 - 6cm
Surinam: Rio Saramacca - system, Goja Creek.

S20060-2 Corydoras sp. "BRAZIL-RONDONIA" juvenil
W, 5 - 6cm
Brazil: Rondonia.

S20403-2 Corydoras sp. C 03 ("deckeri") juvenil   DATZ 12/93
W, 5 - 6cm   (Columbia ?)
Ecuador: Rio Bobonaza+Pindo; Peru: Rio Huallago+Santiago.

S20403-4 Corydoras sp. C 03 ("deckeri") MALE   DATZ 12/93
W, 5 - 6cm   (Columbia ?)
Ecuador: Rio Bobonaza+Pindo; Peru: Rio Huallago+Santiago.

S20403-4 Corydoras sp. C 03 ("deckeri") FEMALE   DATZ 12/93
W, 5 - 6cm   (Columbia ?)
Ecuador: Rio Bobonaza+Pindo; Peru: Rio Huallago+Santiago.

S20419-4 Corydoras sp. C 19 same as C. evelynae I + II DATZ II/94
W, 4 - 5cm
Brazil: Amapa

S20419-4 Corydoras sp. C 19 same as C. evelynae I + II DATZ II/94
W, 4 - 5cm
Brazil: Amapa

S20420-2 Corydoras sp. C 20 "VARIANTE similar C. evelynae
W, 5 - 6 cm DATZ 11/94
Peru

S20426-4 Corydoras sp. C 26 DATZ !/95
W, 5 - 6cm
Brazil: Roaima; Bolivia (?)

S20426-4 Corydoras sp. C 26 DATZ !/95
W, 5 - 6cm
Brazil: Roaima; Bolivia (?)

S20800-4 Corydoras sychri PAIR
W, 5 - 6cm
Surinam: Saramacca District, Rio Coppenam- system.

S20800-4 Corydoras sychri
W, 5 - 6cm
Surinam: Saramacca District, Rio Coppenam- system.

S20800-2 Corydoras sychri semiadult
W, 5 - 6cm
Surinam: Saramacca District, Rio Coppenam- system.

S18200-4 Corydoras agassizii similar C 10
W, 5 - 6cm
Brazil: Amaz.-area near Tabatinga; Peru:Rio Nanay+Napo+Pachitea

S18200-4 Corydoras agassizii similar C 10
W, 5 - 6cm
Brazil: Amaz.-area near Tabatinga; Peru:Rio Nanay+Napo+Pachitea

South America **all Corydoras**

S18210-4 Corydoras sp. aff. agassizii
W, 5 - 6cm
Brazil: Amaz.-area near Tabatinga; Peru:Rio Nanay+Napo+Pachitea

S18205-4 Corydoras agassizii "VARIANTE"
W, 5 - 6cm
Brazil: Amaz.-area near Tabatinga; Peru:Rio Nanay+Napo+Pachitea

S18285-4 Corydoras ambiacus echter/true
Synonym: grafi; melanistius longirostris, W, 4,5 - 6cm
Peru: Edo. Loreto, Rio Ampiyacu+Yavari; Ecuador: Rio Napo-system

S18285-4 Corydoras ambiacus before also C.grafi + mel.longiros.
Synonym: grafi; melanistius longirostris, W, 4,5 - 6cm
Peru: Edo. Loreto, Rio Ampiyacu+Yavari; Ecuador: Rio Napo-system

S18288-4 Corydoras ambiacus "VARIANTE"
Synonym: grafi; melanistius longirostris, W, 4,5 - 6cm
Peru: Edo. Loreto, Rio Ampiyacu+Yavari; Ecuador: Rio Napo-system

S18289-4 Corydoras ambiacus "VARIANTE"
Synonym: grafi; melanistius longirostris, W, 4,5 - 6cm
Peru: Edo. Loreto, Rio Ampiyacu+Yavari; Ecuador: Rio Napo-system

S18290-4 Corydoras cf. ambiacus "SPOTTED II"
Synonym: grafi; melanistius longirostris, W, 4,5 - 6cm
Peru: Edo. Loreto, Rio Ampiyacu+Yavari; Ecuador: Rio Napo-system

S18298-4 Corydoras cf. ambiacus "PERU"
Synonym: grafi; melanistius longirostris, W, 4,5 - 6cm
Peru: Edo. Loreto, Rio Ampiyacu+Yavari; Ecuador: Rio Napo-system

1. **In solchen Biotopen befinden sich Corydoras in Ufernähe.**

   In such biotopes Corydoras can be found near the banks.

2. **Morgendämmerung am Rio Mamoré / Bolivien.**

   Sunrise at the Rio Mamoré / Bolivia.

S20210-4 CORYDORAS sp. "HYBRIDE" (panda x oiapoquensis ?)

S18295-4 Corydoras sp. aff. ambiacus
Synonym: grafi; melanistius longirostris, W, 4,5 - 6cm
Peru: Edo. Loreto, Rio Ampiyacu+Yavari; Ecuador: Rio Napo-system

S18295-4 Corydoras sp. aff. ambiacus
Synonym: grafi; melanistius longirostris, W, 4,5 - 6cm
Peru: Edo. Loreto, Rio Ampiyacu+Yavari; Ecuador: Rio Napo-system

S18295-4 Corydoras sp. aff. ambiacus
Synonym: grafi; melanistius longirostris, W, 4,5 - 6cm
Peru: Edo. Loreto, Rio Ampiyacu+Yavari; Ecuador: Rio Napo-system

S18295-4 Corydoras sp. aff. ambiacus
Synonym: grafi; melanistius longirostris, W, 4,5 - 6cm
Peru: Edo. Loreto, Rio Ampiyacu+Yavari; Ecuador: Rio Napo-system

S18395-4 Corydoras armatus
W, 4,5 - 5cm
Brazil: Est.Amaz.Rio Yavari; Peru: Edo.Loreto,Rio Hullaga +Y avari.

S18395-4 Corydoras armatus
W, 4,5 - 5cm
Brazil: Est.Amaz.Rio Yavari; Peru: Edo.Loreto,Rio Hullaga +Y avari.

S18398-2 Corydoras cf. armatus   semiadult
W, 4,5 - 5cm
Brazil: Est.Amaz.Rio Yavari; Peru: Edo.Loreto,Rio Hullaga +Y avari.

S18398-2 Corydoras cf. armatus   semiadult
W, 4,5 - 5cm
Brazil: Est.Amaz.Rio Yavari; Peru: Edo.Loreto,Rio Hullaga +Y avari.

South America **all Corydoras**

S18765-4 Corydoras delphax
W, 5 - 6cm
Brazil: Rio Unini

S18765-4 Corydoras delphax
W, 5 - 6cm
Brazil: Rio Unini

S18775-4 Corydoras cf. delphax PAIR
W, 5 - 6cm
Brazil: Rio Unini

S18770-4 Corydoras sp. aff. delphax
W, 5 - 6cm
Brazil: Rio Unini

S18770-4 Corydoras sp. aff. delphax
W, 5 - 6cm
Brazil: Rio Unini

S18770-4 Corydoras sp. aff. delphax
W, 5 - 6cm
Brazil: Rio Unini

S18770-4 Corydoras sp. aff. delphax
W, 5 - 6cm
Brazil: Rio Unini

S19080-4 Corydoras incolicana (before C 01)
Synonym: C. "PERAIRA", W, 7 - 8cm
Brazil:Est.Amaz.,upper-course of Rio Negro by Sao Gabriel.

S19080-4 Corydoras incolicana MALE (before C 01)
Synonym: C. "PERAIRA", W, 7 - 8cm
Brazil:Est.Amaz.,upper-course of Rio Negro by Sao Gabriel.

S19080-4 Corydoras incolicana FEMALE (before C 01)
Synonym: C. "PERAIRA", W, 7 - 8cm
Brazil:Est.Amaz.,upper-course of Rio Negro by Sao Gabriel.

S19085-4 Corydoras incolicana "VARIANTE I" (before C 01)
Synonym: C. "PERAIRA", W, 7 - 8cm
Brazil:Est.Amaz.,upper-course of Rio Negro by Sao Gabriel.

S19086-4 Corydoras incolicana "VARIANTE II" (before C 01)
Synonym: C. "PERAIRA", W, 7 - 8cm
Brazil:Est.Amaz.,upper-course of Rio Negro by Sao Gabriel.

S19088-4 Corydoras sp. aff. incolicana (before sp. "PERIRA" C 01)
W, 7 - 8cm
Brazil:Est.Amaz.,upper-course of Rio Negro by Sao Gabriel.

S19150-2 Corydoras leucomelas (before also C.caquetae)
W, 5 - 6cm
Brazil: Est.Para; Ecuador: Napo,Rio Jacuntocha; Peru: Rio Yavari.

S19150-4 Corydoras leucomelas (before also C.caquetae)
W, 5 - 6cm
Brazil: Est.Para; Ecuador: Napo,Rio Jacuntocha; Peru: Rio Yavari.

S19165-4 Corydoras leucomelas "VARIANTE PERU" PAIR
W, 5 - 6cm
Brazil: Est.Para; Ecuador: Napo,Rio Jacuntocha; Peru: Rio Yavari.

S20800-4 CORYDORAS SYCHRI

S18418-4 CORYDORAS ATROPERSONATUS

S19155-4 Corydoras leucomelas "VARIANTE"
W, 5 - 6cm
Brazil: Est.Para; Ecuador: Napo,Rio Jacuntocha; Peru: Rio Yavari.

S19155-4 Corydoras leucomelas "VARIANTE"
W, 5 - 6cm
Brazil: Est.Para; Ecuador: Napo,Rio Jacuntocha; Peru: Rio Yavari.

S19160-4 Corydoras cf. leucomelas
W, 5 - 6cm
Brazil: Est.Para; Ecuador: Napo,Rio Jacuntocha; Peru: Rio Yavari.

S19270-4 Corydoras melanistius melanistius
W, 5 - 5,5cm
Surinam: Brokoponda District; Venezuela: Rio Orinoco.

S19270-4 Corydoras melanistius melanistius
W, 5 - 5,5cm
Surinam: Brokoponda District; Venezuela: Rio Orinoco.

S19270-4 Corydoras melanistius melanistius
W, 5 - 5,5cm
Surinam: Brokoponda District; Venezuela: Rio Orinoco.

S19275-4 Corydoras melanistius melanistius "VARIANTE"
W, 5 - 5,5cm
Surinam: Brokoponda District; Venezuela: Rio Orinoco.

S19280-4 Corydoras cf. melanistius melanistius
W, 5 - 5,5cm
Surinam: Brokoponda District; Venezuela: Rio Orinoco.

South America **all Corydoras**

S19280-4 Corydoras cf. melanistius melanistius
W, 5 - 5,5cm
Surinam: Brokoponda District; Venezuela: Rio Orinoco.

S19281-4 Corydoras cf. melanistius melanistius "SURINAM"
W, 5 - 5,5cm
Surinam: Brokoponda District; Venezuela: Rio Orinoco.

S19250-4 Corydoras melanistius ssp. intergrade I
W, 5 - 5,5cm
Surinam: Brokoponda District; Venezuela: Rio Orinoco.

S19250-4 Corydoras melanistius ssp. intergrade I
W, 5 - 5,5cm
Surinam: Brokoponda District; Venezuela: Rio Orinoco.

S19251-4 Corydoras melanistius ssp. intergrade II
W, 5 - 5,5cm
Surinam: Brokoponda District; Venezuela: Rio Orinoco.

S19251-4 Corydoras melanistius ssp. intergrade II
W, 5 - 5,5cm
Surinam: Brokoponda District; Venezuela: Rio Orinoco.

S19260-4 Corydoras melanistius brevirostris (before C. wotroi)
W, 5 - 6cm
Brazil: Est. Mato Grosso, branch of Rio das Mortes.

S19260-4 Corydoras melanistius brevirostris PAIR
Synonym: wotroi, W, 5 - 6cm
Surinam: Brokoponda District; Venezuela: Rio Orinoco.

S19265-4 Corydoras melanistius brevirostris "VARIANTE" FEMALE
Synonym: wotroi, W, 5 - 6cm
Surinam: Brokoponda District; Venezuela: Rio Orinoco.

S19265-4 Corydoras melanistius brevirostris "VARIANTE" PAIR
Synonym: wotroi, W, 5 - 6cm
Surinam: Brokoponda District; Venezuela: Rio Orinoco.

S19370-4 Corydoras cf. multimaculatus
W, 4 - 5cm
Argentina: Salta (?)

S19375-4 Corydoras sp. aff. multimaculatus
W, 4 - 5cm
Surinam: Brokoponda District; Venezuela: Rio Orinoco.

S19650-4 Corydoras parallelus "C 02" (before sp. CORREAI I)
Synonym: cf.schwartzi; "corrulea", W, 7 - 8cm   DATZ 12/93
Brazil: Rio Icana

S19650-4 Corydoras parallelus "C 02" (before sp. CORREAI I)
Synonym: cf.schwartzi; "corrulea", W, 7 - 8cm   DATZ 12/93
Brazil: Rio Icana

S20080-4 Corydoras sp. "CORREA" (same as C 02 parallelus) MALE
W, 7 - 8cm
Brazil: Rio Icana

S20080-4 Corydoras sp. "CORREA" (same C 02 parallelus) FEMALE
W, 7 - 8cm
Brazil: Rio Icana

South America **all Corydoras**

S20230-4 Corydoras sp. "PERREIRA" similar schwartzi + parallelus
W, 7 - 8cm
Brazil

S20300-4 Corydoras sp. "RIO-NEGRO II" similar C. robustus
W, 5 - 6cm
Brazil: Rio-Negro

S20310-4 Corydoras sp. "RIO-TAPAJOS" similar C.multimaculatus
W, 7 - 8cm
Brazil: Rio Tapajos

S20330-4 Corydoras sp. "RONDONIA" similar C 33 (R 8 in Japan)
W, 6 - 7cm
Brazil: Rondonia

S20370-4 Corydoras sp. "SPOTTED - LONGNOSE" similar C 10
W, 6 - 7cm
Brazil

S20401-4 Corydoras sp. C 01 same/now C. incolicana page 33
W, 7 - 8cm
DATZ 12/93
Brazil: Rio-Icana

S20402-4 Corydoras sp. C 02 same/now C. parallelus page 37
W, 7 - 8cm
DATZ 12/93
Brazil: Rio-Icana

S20406-4 Corydoras sp. C 06 very similar to C.melan.brevirostris
W, 4,5 - 5,5cm
DATZ 12/93
Brazil: Rio-Guama

S20760-4 CORYDORAS SURINAMENSIS

S20409-4 Corydoras sp. C 09   DATZ 12/93
    W, 4,5 - 5cm
    Venezuela: Rio Caroni.Peru(?)

S20409-3 Corydoras sp. C 09 "RIO-UTIQUINEA PERU" DATZ 12/93
    W, 4,5 - 5cm
    Venezuela: Rio Caroni.Peru(?)

S20410-4 Corydoras sp. C 10   similar C. agassizii   DATZ 12/93
    W, 5 - 6cm
    Columbia; Brazil(?).

S20418-4 Corydoras sp. C 18   similar C.julii, leopardus, trillineatus
    W, 4,5 - 5,5cm   DATZ 4/94
    Brazil: Rondonia.

S20421-4 Corydoras sp. C 21   DATZ 12/94
    W, 5 - 6cm
    Brazil: Amapa; Rio-Xingu(?)

S20421-4 Corydoras sp. C 21   DATZ 12/94
    W, 5 - 6cm
    Brazil: Amapa; Rio-Xingu(?).

S20430-4 Corydoras sp. C 30   similar to C. melanistius brevirostr.
    W, 4 - 5cm   DATZ 4/95
    Brazil: Amapa

S20433-4 Corydoras sp. C 33 "VARIANTE"   DATZ 8/95
    W, 5 - 6cm
    Brazil: Rondonia

S20434-4 Corydoras sp. C 34 Roraima/Brazil DATZ 8/95
W, 5 - 6cm
Brazil: Rondonia

S20434-4 Corydoras sp. C 34 same/similar C. sp. "RED-CHEEK"
W, 5 - 6cm DATZ 8/95
Brazil: Rondonia

S20434-4 Corydoras sp. C 34 "VARIANTE" pathogen DATZ 8/95
W, 5 - 6cm
Brazil: Rondonia

S20443-4 Corydoras sp. C 43 DATZ 3/96
W, 4 - 5cm
Herkunft nicht bekannt / origin unknown !

S20444-4 Corydoras sp. C 44 DATZ 3/96
W, 5 - 6cm
Peru

S20446-4 Corydoras sp. C 46 similar C. sp. "RIO-BRANCO" PAIR
W, 5 - 6cm DATZ 3/96
Peru: Rio-Branco

S20760-2 Corydoras surinamensis semiadult
Synonym: schwartzi surinamensis, W, 4 - 5cm
Brazil: Mata Grosso.

S20770-4 Corydoras cf. surinamensis
Synonym: schwartzi surinamensis, W, 4 - 5cm
Brazil: Mata Grosso.

South America **all Corydoras**

S19810-1 CORYDORAS ROBINEAE "babies 4 weeks old"

S20770-4 Corydoras cf. surinamensis (sp. BLACKFIN) MALE
Synonym: schwartzi surinamensis, W, 4 - 5cm
Brazil: Mata Grosso.

S20770-4 Corydoras cf. surinamensis (sp. BLACKFIN) FEMALE
Synonym: schwartzi surinamensis, W, 4 - 5cm
Brazil: Mata Grosso.

S20770-4 Corydoras cf. surinamensis
Synonym: schwartzi surinamensis, W, 4 - 5cm
Brazil: Mata Grosso.

S19530-4 Corydoras ornatus "WHITE-TOP"
W, 5 - 6cm
Franz.Guyana: Cumuri Creek branch of Rio Oyapock, Campori-River

S19535-4 Corydoras cf. ornatus
W, 5 - 6cm
Franz.Guyana: Cumuri Creek branch of Rio Oyapock, Campori-River

S19537-4 Corydoras sp. aff. ornatus
W, 5 - 6cm
Franz.Guyana: Cumuri Creek branch of Rio Oyapock, Campori-River

S19722-4 Corydoras pulcher "VARIANTE I"
W, 6 - 7cm
Brazil: Est. Espirita Santo, Sao Jao de Petropolis.

S19722-4 Corydoras pulcher "VARIANTE I"
W, 6 - 7cm
Brazil: Est. Espirita Santo, Sao Jao de Petropolis.

South America **all Corydoras**

S19722-4 Corydoras pulcher "VARIANTE I" MALE
W, 6 - 7cm
Brazil: Est. Espirita Santo, Sao Jao de Petropolis.

S19723-4 Corydoras pulcher "VARIANTE II"
W, 6 - 7cm
Brazil: Est. Espirita Santo, Sao Jao de Petropolis.

S19724-4 Corydoras pulcher "VARIANTE III"
W, 6 - 7cm
Brazil: Est. Espirita Santo, Sao Jao de Petropolis.

S19820-4 Corydoras robustus
W, 7 - 8cm
Brazil: middle-course of Rio Negro, Rio Aiuana.

S19820-4 Corydoras robustus   MALE
W, 7 - 8cm
Brazil: middle-course of Rio Negro, Rio Aiuana.

S19820-4 Corydoras robustus   FEMALE
W, 7 - 8cm
Brazil: middle-course of Rio Negro, Rio Aiuana.

S19860-4 Corydoras schwartzi Original-Erstbeschr. Rössel
W, 5 - 6cm   see DATZ 11/93
Brazil: Est. Nato Grosso, Rio Sarare, branch of Rio Guapore.

S19860-4 Corydoras schwartzi
W, 5 - 6cm
Brazil: middle-course of Rio Negro, Rio Aiuana.

S19860-4 Corydoras schwartzi
W, 5 - 6cm
Brazil: middle-course of Rio Negro, Rio Aiuana.

S19862-4 Corydoras schwartzi VARIANTE I
W, 5 - 6cm
Brazil: middle-course of Rio Negro, Rio Aiuana.

S19863-4 Corydoras schwartzi VARIANTE II
W, 5 - 6cm
Brazil: middle-course of Rio Negro, Rio Aiuana.

S19865-4 Corydoras schwartzi VARIANTE III
W, 5 - 6cm
Brazil: middle-course of Rio Negro, Rio Aiuana.

S19866-4 Corydoras schwartzi VARIANTE IV very simil. C.pulcher
W, 5 - 6cm
Brazil: middle-course of Rio Negro, Rio Aiuana.

S19867-4 Corydoras schwartzi VARIANTE V "LONGNOSE"
W, 5 - 6cm
Brazil: middle-course of Rio Negro, Rio Aiuana.

S19868-4 Corydoras schwartzi VARIANTE VI "LONGNOSE"
W, 5 - 6cm
Brazil: middle-course of Rio Negro, Rio Aiuana.

S20040-4 Corydoras sp. "BRAZIL" similar C.schwartzi Variante III
W, 5,5 - 6,5cm
Brazil

South America **all Corydoras**

S20110-4 Coydoras sp. "FALSO-ROBUSTUS"
  W, 5 - 6cm
  Brazil (?)

S20290-4 Corydoras sp. "RIO-NEGRO I" similar C.multimaculatus
  W, 5 - 6cm
  Brazil: Rio Negro.

S20360-4 Corydoras sp. "SPOTTED-LINE" similar to C.schwartzi
  W, 5 - 6cm
  Brazil

S20380-4 Corydoras sp. "THREE-SPOT:-LINES" simil.C.schwartzi
  W, 5 - 6cm
  Brazil

S20250-4 Corydoras sp. "PERU" similar to C. C 18
  W, 5 - 6cm
  Peru

S18320-4 Corydoras araguaiaensis
  W, 5 - 6cm
Brazil: Est. Mato Grosso, Rio Araguaia.

S18320-4 Corydoras araguaiaensis   PAIR
  W, 5 - 6cm
Brazil: Est. Mato Grosso, Rio Araguaia.

S18320-4 Corydoras araguaiaensis
  W, 5 - 6cm
Brazil: Est. Mato Grosso, Rio Araguaia.

S20840-4 CORYDORAS TRILINEATUS PAIR

S18320-4 Corydoras araguaiaensis   MALE
W, 5 - 6cm
Brazil: Est. Mato Grosso, Rio Araguaia.

S18325-4 Corydoras araguaiaensis VARIANTE I
W, 5 - 6cm
Brazil: Est. Mato Grosso, Rio Araguaia.

S18326-4 Corydoras araguaiaensis VARIANTE II "BIG-SPOT" MALE
W, 5 - 6cm
Brazil: Est. Mato Grosso, Rio Araguaia.

S18326-4 Corydoras araguaiaensis VARIAN. II"BIG-SPOT" FEMALE
W, 5 - 6cm
Brazil: Est. Mato Grosso, Rio Araguaia.

S18960-4 Corydoras sp. aff. geryi   same as C 11
W, 4 - 5cm
Brazil: Est. Bahia, Rio Sao Francisco; Est. Ceara, Rio Granjeiro.

S18970-4 Corydoras gomezi
W, 5 - 6cm
Bolivia: Provinz Beni, Rio Mamore-systemby Trinidad.

S18970-4 Corydoras gomezi
W, 5 - 6cm
Bolivia: Provinz Beni, Rio Mamore-systemby Trinidad.

S19030-4 Corydoras haraldschultzi
W, 7 - 8cm
Columbia: Rio Casanare; Ven: Edo Cojedes,Rio Salinas + Pajo Viejo.

S19030-4 Corydoras haraldschultzi
W, 7 - 8cm
Columbia: Rio Casanare; Ven: Edo Cojedes, Rio Salinas + Pajo Viejo.

S19030-4 Corydoras haraldschultzi
W, 7 - 8cm
Columbia: Rio Casanare; Ven: Edo Cojedes, Rio Salinas + Pajo Viejo.

S19095-4 Corydoras julii PAIR
W, 4,5 - 5cm
Brazil: Rio Icana, branch of Rio Negro.

S19095-4 Corydoras julii PAIR
W, 4,5 - 5cm
Brazil: Rio Icana, branch of Rio Negro.

S19098-4 Corydoras julii VARIANTE I
W, 4,5 - 5cm
Brazil: Rio Icana, branch of Rio Negro.

S19099-4 Corydoras julii VARIANTE II
W, 4,5 - 5cm
Brazil: Rio Icana, branch of Rio Negro.

S19135-4 Corydoras leopardus
Synonym: funnelli, W, 5 - 6cm
Bolivia: Provinz Beni, Rio Beni-system, Lago Rogoagua.

S19138-4 Corydoras leopardus "VARIANTE"
Synonym: funnelli, W, 5 - 6cm
Bolivia: Provinz Beni, Rio Beni-system, Lago Rogoagua.

South America **all Corydoras**

S19720-4 CORYDORAS PULCHER

S19860-4 CORYDORAS SCHWARTZI

S19210-4 Corydoras maculifer
W, 6,5 - 7cm
Brazil: Est. Parana, Paranaqua.

S19210-4 Corydoras maculifer
W, 6,5 - 7cm
Brazil: Est. Parana, Paranaqua.

S19210-1 Corydoras maculifer babies 17 days old
W, 6,5 - 7cm
Brazil: Est. Parana, Paranaqua.

S19210-2 Corydoras maculifer semiadult
W, 6,5 - 7cm
Brazil: Est. Parana, Paranaqua.

S19555-4 Corydoras osteocarus MALE adult
W, 3,5 - 4cm
Ecuador: Edo Pastaza, upper-course of Rio Bobonaza.

S19555-1 Corydoras osteocarus babies 3 weeks old !
W, 3,5 - 4cm
Ecuador: Edo Pastaza, upper-course of Rio Bobonaza.

S19680-4 Corydoras pinheiroi "C 25"
W, 5 - 6cm
Brazil: Rondonia

S19810-3 Corydoras robineae
W, 6,5 - 7cm
Columbia: Prov.Caqueta, tributary of Rio Orteguaza by TresEquinas

S19810-4 Corydoras robineae
W, 6,5 - 7cm
Columbia: Prov.Caqueta, tributary of Rio Orteguaza by TresEquinas

S19810-4 Corydoras robineae   PAIR
W, 6,5 - 7cm
Columbia: Prov.Caqueta, tributary of Rio Orteguaza by TresEquinas

S20070-4 Corydoras sp. "BRAZIL - SHARPHEAD"
(it's not C. copei, but similar C. leopardus !) W, 5 - 6cm
Brazil

S20260-4 Corydoras sp. "PERU I" (similar to C. copei, but not true!)
very similar to C. julii ! W, 3,5 - 4,5cm

S20411-4 Corydoras sp. C 11 same/now C. sp. aff. geryi, page 48 !
W, 4 - 5cm   DATZ 12/93
Brazil / Bolivia (Peru ?)

S20412-4 Corydoras sp. C 12 similar C.leopardus + orphnopterus
W, 4,5 - 5cm   DATZ 12/93
Bolivia / Brazil

S20413-4 Corydoras sp. C 13
W, 4,5 - 5cm
Brazil: Rio Xingu; Columbia(?)

S19680-4 Corydoras sp. C 25 same/now C. pinheiroi pg.51
W, 5 - 6cm   DATZ 1/95
Brazil: Rondonia

S20750-4 Corydoras sterbai   MALE
  W, 5,5 - 6cm
Peru: Rio Ucayali, Yarina Cocha, and more rivers to Ucayali-system.

S20750-4 Corydoras sterbai   FEMALE
  W, 5,5 - 6cm
Peru: Rio Ucayali, Yarina Cocha, and more rivers to Ucayali-system.

S20750-4 Corydoras sterbai   ablaichendes Paar / spawning pair !
  B, 5,5 - 6cm
Peru: Rio Ucayali, Yarina Cocha, and more rivers to Ucayali-system.

S20750-4 Corydoras sterbai   WEIBCHEN mit Eiern in Bauchtasche!
  B, 5,5 - 6cm   FEMALE with eggs in belly-touch !
Peru: Rio Ucayali, Yarina Cocha, and more rivers to Ucayali-system.

S20750-4 Corydoras sterbai   Eier deponierendes WEIBCHEN !
  B, 5,5 - 6cm   Eggs depositing FEMALE !
Peru: Rio Ucayali, Yarina Cocha, and more rivers to Ucayali-system.

-------- Corydoras sterbai   "GELEGE / SPAWN-HATCHING"

S20750-1 Corydoras sterbai   "BABIES 3-4 weeks old !
  B, 5,5 - 6cm
Peru: Rio Ucayali, Yarina Cocha, and more rivers to Ucayali-system.

S20750-2 Corydoras sterbai   "JUVENIL 7-8 weeks old !
  B, 5,5 - 6cm
Peru: Rio Ucayali, Yarina Cocha, and more rivers to Ucayali-system.

South America **all Corydoras**

S18690-4 CORYDORAS CONDISCIPULUS

1. Trigonectes strigabundus
2. Nothobranchius jubbi

Diese und alle anderen demnächst in
These and all others coming soon in

"Killi`s of the **world**"

S20445-4 Corydoras sp. C 45 same C. cf. araguaiaensis "BIG-SPOT"
W, 5 - 6cm
Columbia   DATZ 3/96

S20840-4 Corydoras trilineatus
Synonym: dubius; episcopi, W, 4,5 - 5cm
Brazil: Est. Maranhao, Rio Parnahyba by Viktoria.

S20840-4 Corydoras trilineatus   PAIR
Synonym: dubius; episcopi, W, 4,5 - 5cm
Brazil: Est. Maranhao, Rio Parnahyba by Viktoria.

S20845-4 Corydoras trilineatus   "VARIANTE"
Synonym: dubius; episcopi, W, 4,5 - 5cm
Brazil: Est. Maranhao, Rio Parnahyba by Viktoria.

S19775-4 Corydoras reticulatus
W, 5 - 6cm
Brazil: Est.Amazonas, Rio Javari; Peru: Rio Yavari + Rio Ucayali.

S19775-4 Corydoras reticulatus
W, 5 - 6cm
Brazil: Est.Amazonas, Rio Javari; Peru: Rio Yavari + Rio Ucayali.

S19775-4 Corydoras reticulatus   PAIR
W, 5 - 6cm
Brazil: Est.Amazonas, Rio Javari; Peru: Rio Yavari + Rio Ucayali.

S19778-4 Corydoras reticulatus   "VARIANTE"
W, 5 - 6cm
Brazil: Est.Amazonas, Rio Javari; Peru: Rio Yavari + Rio Ucayali.

South America **all Corydoras**

S20000-4 Corydoras sodalis
W, 5,5 - 6cm
Columbia: Rio Meta, Rio Ocoa by Puerto Lopez.

S20000-4 Corydoras sodalis
W, 5,5 - 6cm
Columbia: Rio Meta, Rio Ocoa by Puerto Lopez.

S20003-4 Corydoras sodalis "HOCHRÜCKEN / HIGH-BODY"
W, 5,5 - 6cm
Columbia: Rio Meta, Rio Ocoa by Puerto Lopez.

S20004-4 Corydoras sodalis "GESTRECKT / LOW-BODY"
W, 5,5 - 6cm
Columbia: Rio Meta, Rio Ocoa by Puerto Lopez.

S20000-4 Corydoras sodalis PAIR
W, 5,5 - 6cm
Columbia: Rio Meta, Rio Ocoa by Puerto Lopez.

S20000-4 Corydoras sodalis
W, 5,5 - 6cm
Columbia: Rio Meta, Rio Ocoa by Puerto Lopez.

S20008-4 Corydoras sodalis "ROUND-HEAD"
W, 5,5 - 6cm
Columbia: Rio Meta, Rio Ocoa by Puerto Lopez.

S20005-4 Corydoras sodalis "VARIANTE GREY"
W, 5,5 - 6cm
Columbia: Rio Meta, Rio Ocoa by Puerto Lopez.

South America **all Corydoras**

S18650-4 Corydoras cervinus
W, 5 - 6cm
Brazil: Est. Rondonia, upper-course of Rio Guapore.

S18650-4 Corydoras cervinus
W, 5 - 6cm
Brazil: Est. Rondonia, upper-course of Rio Guapore.

S18652-4 Corydoras cervinus   HELL / LIGHT A
W, 5 - 6cm
Brazil: Est. Rondonia, upper-course of Rio Guapore.

S19953-4 Corydoras cervinus   HELL / LIGHT B
W, 5 - 6cm
Brazil: Est. Rondonia, upper-course of Rio Guapore.

S20424-4 Corydoras sp. C 24 similar C. cervinus
W, 5 - 6cm   DATZ 12/94
Brazil: Rio-Guama

S20424-4 Corydoras sp. C 24 similar C. cervinus
W, 5 - 6cm   DATZ 12/94
Brazil: Rio-Guama

S20428-4 Corydoras sp. C 28 similar C. cervinus + blochi
W, 5 - 6cm   DATZ 4/95
Brazil: Rondonia

S20442-4 Corydoras sp. C 42 ("KRISTINAE") very similar C 24
W, 5 - 6cm   DATZ 3/96
Brazil: Rio-Guama by Ourem

S19775-4 CORYDORAS RETICULATUS

S20000-4 CORYDORAS SODALIS

S19690-4 Corydoras polystictus MALE
Synonym: virescens, W, 4 - 4,5cm
Brazil: Est.,Rondonia, branch of Rio Ribeiro by Guajara-Mirim.

S19690-4 Corydoras polystictus FEMALE
Synonym: virescens, W, 4 - 4,5cm
Brazil: Est.,Rondonia, branch of Rio Ribeiro by Guajara-Mirim.

S19690-4 Corydoras polystictus
Synonym: virescens, W, 4 - 4,5cm
Brazil: Est.,Rondonia, branch of Rio Ribeiro by Guajara-Mirim.

S19695-4 Corydoras polystictus   "VARIANTE"
Synonym: virescens, W, 4 - 4,5cm
Brazil: Est.,Rondonia, branch of Rio Ribeiro by Guajara-Mirim.

S19690-4 Corydoras polystictus   PAIR (before also C. virescens)
Synonym: virescens, W, 4 - 4,5cm
Brazil: Est.,Rondonia, branch of Rio Ribeiro by Guajara-Mirim.

S19692-4 Corydoras polystictus   "XANTHORIST / YELLOW"
Synonym: virescens, W, 4 - 4,5cm
Brazil: Est.,Rondonia, branch of Rio Ribeiro by Guajara-Mirim.

S19970-4 Corydoras similis PAIR
W, 4,5 - 5cm
Brazil: Rondonia.

S19970-4 Corydoras similis
W, 4,5 - 5cm
Brazil: Rondonia.

S20150-4 Corydoras sp. "GOLD" FEMALE very similar C.paleatus
W, 6 - 7cm (see DATZ 12/94)
Paraguay (?)

S20150-2 Corydoras sp. "GOLD" JUVENIL very similar C.paleatus
W, 6 - 7cm (see DATZ 12/94)
Paraguay (?)

S20414-2 Corydoras sp. C 14 similar C. sanchesi   DATZ 12/93
W, 4,5 - 5cm
Brazil: Rio Xingu; Venezuela: Rio-Coroni(?)

S20415-4 Corydoras sp. aff. C 14 ("RIO-BRANCO") MALE
W, 4 - 5cm
Brazil: Rio Branco (?)

S20415-4 Corydoras sp. aff. C 14 ("RIO-BRANCO") FEMALE
W, 4 - 5cm
Brazil: Rio Branco (?)

S21000-4 Corydoras xinguensis PAIR
W, 3,5 - 4cm
Peru: Est. Ouzco, branch of Rio Vilcanota.

S21000-4 Corydoras xinguensis
W, 3,5 - 4cm
Peru: Est. Ouzco, branch of Rio Vilcanota.

S21003-4 Corydoras xinguensis VARIANTE A
W, 3,5 - 4cm
Peru: Est. Ouzco, branch of Rio Vilcanota.

South America **all Corydoras**

S18355-4 CORYDORAS ARCUATUS PAIR

S19410-4 CORYDORAS NARCISSUS

S19005-4 Corydoras cf. griseus very similar C 40
Synonym: griseus deweyeri, W, 4,5 - 5cm
Brazil: Est.Para, Rio Madeira+Tapajos, branch 66,5km from Itaituba.

S19005-4 Corydoras cf. griseus very similar C 40
Synonym: griseus deweyeri, W, 4,5 - 5cm
Brazil: Est.Para, Rio Madeira+Tapajos, branch 66,5km from Itaituba.

S19510-4 Corydoras oiapoquensis
W, 4 - 5cm,   Distr.Marowijne, Marowijne river-system;
Surinam: Distr.Brokopondo, Surinam river-system.

S19511-4 Corydoras oiapoquensis VARIANTE A
W, 4 - 5cm,   Distr.Marowijne, Marowijne river-system;
Surinam: Distr.Brokopondo, Surinam river-system.

S19512-4 Corydoras oiapoquensis VARIANTE B
W, 4 - 5cm,   Distr.Marowijne, Marowijne river-system;
Surinam: Distr.Brokopondo, Surinam river-system.

S19513-4 Corydoras oiapoquensis VARIANTE C
W, 4 - 5cm,   Distr.Marowijne, Marowijne river-system;
Surinam: Distr.Brokopondo, Surinam river-system.

S19514-4 Corydoras oiapoquensis VARIANTE D
W, 4 - 5cm,   Distr.Marowijne, Marowijne river-system;
Surinam: Distr.Brokopondo, Surinam river-system.

S19510-1 Corydoras oiapoquensis BABIES 4 weeks old !
W, 4 - 5cm,   Distr.Marowijne, Marowijne river-system;
Surinam: Distr.Brokopondo, Surinam river-system.

S19515-4 Corydoras sp. aff. oiapoquensis "PLANE-TAIL"
W, 4 - 5cm, Distr.Marowijne, Marowijne river-system;
Surinam: Distr.Brokopondo, Surinam river-system.

S19700-4 Corydoras cf. potaroensis
W, 4 - 5cm
Brazil: Est. Mato Grosso, Rio Guapore, Rio Paraguaya.

S19700-4 Corydoras cf. potaroensis
W, 4 - 5cm
Brazil: Est. Mato Grosso, Rio Guapore, Rio Paraguaya.

S20440-4 Corydoras sp. C 40 very similar C.cf.griseus RONDONIA
pg.66   W, 4,5 - 5cm   DATZ 3/96
Brazil: Rondonia

S18230-4 Corydoras amandajanea similar C.crypticus + burgessi
W, 5 - 6cm
Brazil: Rio Miua-system, upper-course of Rio-Negro.

S18235-4 Corydoras amandajanea similar C.crypticus + burgessi
VARIANTE "STRONG-PIGMENT" W, 5 - 6cm
Brazil: Rio Miua-system, upper-course of Rio-Negro.

S18245-4 Corydoras sp. aff. amandajanea
W, 5 - 6cm   similar C.crypticus + burgessi
Brazil: Rio Miua-system, upper-course of Rio-Negro.

S18355-4 Corydoras arcuatus
W, 5 - 6cm
Brazil: Rio Humaita; Ecuador: Rio Napo-system; Peru: Rio Pacaya.

South America **all Corydoras**

S18355-4 Corydoras arcuatus adult!
  W, 5 - 6cm
Brazil: Rio Humaita; Ecuador: Rio Napo-system; Peru: Rio Pacaya.

S18355-2 Corydoras arcuatus juvenil!
  W, 5 - 6cm
Brazil: Rio Humaita; Ecuador: Rio Napo-system; Peru: Rio Pacaya.

S18375-4 Corydoras arcuatus "SUPER-ARCUATUS" same as C 20
  W, 7 - 8cm
Brazil: Rio Humaita; Ecuador: Rio Napo-system; Peru: Rio Pacaya.

S18375-2 Corydoras arcuatus "SUPER-ARCUATUS" same as C 20
  W, 7 - 8cm
Brazil: Rio Humaita; Ecuador: Rio Napo-system; Peru: Rio Pacaya.

S18365-4 Corydoras sp. aff. arcuatus "BROKEN-STRIPE"
  W, 7 - 8cm
Brazil: Rio Humaita; Ecuador: Rio Napo-system; Peru: Rio Pacaya.

S18545-4 Corydoras bicolor
  W, 3 - 4cm
Surinam: Corantijn-system, Sipaliwini-river, Lucie-river.

S18555-4 Corydoras sp. aff. bicolor
  W, 3 - 4cm
Surinam: Corantijn-system, Sipaliwini-river, Lucie-river.

S18600-4 Corydoras burgessi
  W, 5 - 6cm
Brazil: Rio Unini, branch of Rio Negro.

South America **all Corydoras**   © Verlag A.C.S. GmbH

3 FISHES: Corydoras burgessi, Corydoras adolfoi, Corydoras nijsseni (all fr. l. - r.)

links/left: CORYDORAS METAE + rechts/right: CORYDORAS DAVIDSANDSI

S18600-4 Corydoras burgessi
W, 5 - 6cm
Brazil: Rio Unini, branch of Rio Negro.

S18604-4 Corydoras burgessi VARIANTE SPOTTED MALE
W, 5 - 6cm
Brazil: Rio Unini, branch of Rio Negro.

S18600-4 Corydoras burgessi MALE
W, 5 - 6cm
Brazil: Rio Unini, branch of Rio Negro.

S18600-4 Corydoras burgessi FEMALE
W, 5 - 6cm
Brazil: Rio Unini, branch of Rio Negro.

S18605-4 Corydoras burgessi VARIANTE "STRIPED" MALE
W, 5 - 6cm
Brazil: Rio Unini, branch of Rio Negro.

S18605-4 Corydoras burgessi VARIANTE "STRIPED" FEMALE
W, 5 - 6cm
Brazil: Rio Unini, branch of Rio Negro.

S18602-4 Corydoras burgessi VARIANTE "SPOTTED" s.DATZ 3/95 BREEDING-FORM
B, 5 - 6cm
Brazil: Rio Unini, branch of Rio Negro.

S18615-4 Corydoras sp. aff. burgessi
W, 5 - 6cm
Brazil: Rio Unini, branch of Rio Negro.

South America **all Corydoras**

S18745-4 Corydoras crypticus
W, 4 - 5cm
Columbia: Rio Arauca by Arauca.

S18747-4 Corydoras crypticus "SPOTTED"
W, 4 - 5cm
Columbia: Rio Arauca by Arauca.

S18746-4 Corydoras crypticus HYBRIDE (?)
W, 4 - 5cm
Columbia: Rio Arauca by Arauca.

S18775-4 Corydoras sp. aff. crypticus
W, 4 - 5cm
Columbia: Rio Arauca by Arauca.

S20160-4 Corydoras sp. HYBRIDE burgessi x (?) natur!
W, 5 - 6cm
Brazil

S20170-4 Corydoras sp. HYBRIDE burgessi x adolfoi
W, 5 - 6cm
Brazil

S20180-4 Corydoras sp. HYBRIDE burgessi x davidsandsi
5 - 6cm
Brazil

S20200-4 Corydoras sp. HYBRIDE panda x davidsandsi
5 - 6cm
Brazil (?); Peru (?)

South America **all Corydoras**

S18040-4 Corydoras adolfoi HYBRIDE
6 - 7cm   probably natur-hybride: adolfoi x virginiae (?)
Brazil (?)

S18041-4 Corydoras adolfoi HYBRIDE
6 - 7cm probably natur-hybride: virginiae x adolfoi (?)
Brazil (?)

S20940-4 Corydoras virginiae C 04   DATZ 12/93
Synonym: "miguelita", (before C 04) W, 5 - 6cm
Argentina: La Plata-Region by Buenos Aires; Peru(?)

S20940-4 Corydoras virginiae C 04   DATZ 12/93
Synonym: "miguelita", (before C 04) W, 5 - 6cm
Argentina: La Plata-Region by Buenos Aires; Peru(?)

S20942-4 Corydoras virginiae VARIANTE C 04   DATZ 12/93
Synonym: "miguelita", (before C 04) W, 5 - 6cm
Argentina: La Plata-Region by Buenos Aires; Peru(?)

S20950-4 Corydoras virginiae VARIANTE (HYBRIDE ? DATZ 12/93
Synonym: "miguelita", (before C 04) W, 5 - 6cm
Argentina: La Plata-Region by Buenos Aires; Peru(?)

S18025-4 Corydoras adolfoi
W, 6 - 7cm
Brazil: uppere-course of Rio Negro by Sao Gabriel de Cachoeira.

S18025-4 Corydoras adolfoi   PAIR
W, 6 - 7cm
Brazil: uppere-course of Rio Negro by Sao Gabriel de Cachoeira.

South America **all Corydoras**

S18025-4 Corydoras adolfoi FEMALE with babies !
B, 5 - 6cm
Brazil: uppere-course of Rio Negro by Sao Gabriel de Cachoeira.

S18025-1 Corydoras adolfoi BABY-SCHOOL !
B, 5 - 6cm
Brazil: uppere-course of Rio Negro by Sao Gabriel de Cachoeira.

S18035-4 Corydoras adolfoi VARIANTE SPOTTED MALE
W, 5 - 6cm
Brazil: uppere-course of Rio Negro by Sao Gabriel de Cachoeira.

S18035-4 Corydoras adolfoi VARIANTE SPOTTED FEMALE
W, 5 - 6cm
Brazil: uppere-course of Rio Negro by Sao Gabriel de Cachoeira.

S18790-4 Corydoras duplicareus MALE
W, 4 - 5cm
Columbia: Rio Inirida-system + Rio Orinoco-system.

S18790-4 Corydoras duplicareus FEMALE
W, 4 - 5cm
Columbia: Rio Inirida-system + Rio Orinoco-system.

S19055-4 Corydoras imitator very similar C. serratus see page 79
W, 6 - 7cm
Surinam: Coppename-river + Nickerie-river.

S19055-4 Corydoras imitator PAIR
W, 6 - 7cm
Surinam: Coppename-river + Nickerie-river.

South America **all Corydoras** © Verlag A.C.S. GmbH

S19450-4 Corydoras nijsseni MALE
Synonym: elegans nijsseni, W, 4,5 - 5cm
Brazil: Est. Amazonas, branches of upper Rio Negro.

S19450-4 Corydoras nijsseni FEMALE
Synonym: elegans nijsseni, W, 4,5 - 5cm
Brazil: Est. Amazonas, branches of upper Rio Negro.

S19450-4 Corydoras nijsseni   PAIR
Synonym: elegans nijsseni, W, 4,5 - 5cm
Brazil: Est. Amazonas, branches of upper Rio Negro.

S19450-4 Corydoras nijsseni FEMALE
Synonym: elegans nijsseni, W, 4,5 - 5cm
Brazil: Est. Amazonas, branches of upper Rio Negro.

S19452-4 Corydoras nijsseni VARIANTE SPOTTED MALE
Synonym: elegans nijsseni, W, 4,5 - 5cm
Brazil: Est. Amazonas, branches of upper Rio Negro.

S19452-4 Corydoras nijsseni VARIANTE SPOTTED   FEMALE
Synonym: elegans nijsseni, W, 4,5 - 5cm
Brazil: Est. Amazonas, branches of upper Rio Negro.

S19454-4 Corydoras nijsseni VARIANTE BROADBAND MALE
Synonym: elegans nijsseni, W, 4,5 - 5cm
Brazil: Est. Amazonas, branches of upper Rio Negro.

S19454-4 Corydoras nijsseni VARIANTE BROADBAND   FEMALE
Synonym: elegans nijsseni, W, 4,5 - 5cm
Brazil: Est. Amazonas, branches of upper Rio Negro.

S19455-4 Corydoras nijsseni VARIANTE BLACK MALE
Synonym: elegans nijsseni, W, 4,5 - 5cm
Brazil: Est. Amazonas, branches of upper Rio Negro.

S19455-4 Corydoras nijsseni VARIANTE BLACK FEMALE
Synonym: elegans nijsseni, W, 4,5 - 5cm
Brazil: Est. Amazonas, branches of upper Rio Negro.

S19470-4 Corydoras sp. aff. nijsseni LONGNOSE
Synonym: elegans nijsseni, W, 4,5 - 5cm
Brazil: Est. Amazonas, branches of upper Rio Negro.

S19470-4 Corydoras sp. aff. nijsseni LONGNOSE
Synonym: elegans nijsseni, W, 4,5 - 5cm
Brazil: Est. Amazonas, branches of upper Rio Negro.

S20439-4 Corydoras sp. C 39 similar C. davidsandsi, but longnose!
W, 5 - 6cm   DATZ 3/96

S19410-4 Corydoras narcissus TYPUSLOCALITY !!!
W, 6 - 7cm
Ecuador: Rio Aguairico+Napo-system; Peru: Rio Nanay by Iquitos.

S19410-4 Corydoras narcissus
W, 6 - 7cm
Ecuador: Rio Aguairico+Napo-system; Peru: Rio Nanay by Iquitos.

S19410-4 Corydoras narcissus PAIR
W, 6 - 7cm
Ecuador: Rio Aguairico+Napo-system; Peru: Rio Nanay by Iquitos.

S18755-4 Corydoras davidsandsi MALE
W, 5,5 - 6cm
Brazil: Rio Miua-system, 12km before mouth to Rio Negro.

S18755-4 Corydoras davidsandsi FEMALE
W, 5,5 - 6cm
Brazil: Rio Miua-system, 12km before mouth to Rio Negro.

S19315-4 Corydoras melini
W, 4,5 - 5cm
Columbia: Provinz Honda, Rio Magdalena-area, Tolima.

S19315-4 Corydoras melini PAIR
W, 4,5 - 5cm
Columbia: Provinz Honda, Rio Magdalena-area, Tolima.

S19340-4 Corydoras metae PAIR
W, 4,5 - 5cm
Columbia: Rio Papuri+Vaupes com.tog.; Ecuador: Canambo+Pindo

S19340-4 Corydoras metae FEMALE
W, 4,5 - 5cm
Columbia: Rio Papuri+Vaupes com.tog.; Ecuador: Canambo+Pindo

S19342-4 Corydoras metae VARIANTE MALE
W, 4,5 - 5cm
Columbia: Rio Papuri+Vaupes com.tog.; Ecuador: Canambo+Pindo

S19342-4 Corydoras metae VARIANTE FEMALE
W, 4,5 - 5cm
Columbia: Rio Papuri+Vaupes com.tog.; Ecuador: Canambo+Pindo

South America **all Corydoras**

S19630-2 Corydoras panda "BIG-SPOT"
W, 4,5 - 5cm
Peru

S19635-4 Corydoras panda "SMALL-SPOT"
W, 4,5 - 5cm
Peru

S19980-4 Corydoras simulatus
W, 6 - 7cm
Brazil: Est.Rondonia, branche to Rio Madeira by Ariqumes.

S19980-4 Corydoras simulatus
W, 6 - 7cm
Brazil: Est.Rondonia, branche to Rio Madeira by Ariqumes.

S19980-1 Corydoras simulatus   BABY + JUVENIL
W, 6 - 7cm
Brazil: Est.Rondonia, branche to Rio Madeira by Ariqumes.

S19983-4 Corydoras simulatus   VARIANTE
W, 6 - 7cm
Brazil: Est.Rondonia, branche to Rio Madeira by Ariqumes.

S20416-4 Corydoras sp. C 16   DATZ 4/94
W, 5 - 6cm
Brazil: Mato Grosso; (Import from Columbia ??)

S20416-4 Corydoras sp. C 16   DATZ 4/94
W, 5 - 6cm
Brazil: Mato Grosso; (Import from Columbia ??)

S19935-4 Corydoras serratus   same as C 29
W, 5 - 6cm
Venezuela: Rio Pina(north Maturin), Rio Amana + Tinaquilla.

S19935-4 Corydoras serratus   same as C 29
W, 5 - 6cm
Venezuela: Rio Pina(north Maturin), Rio Amana + Tinaquilla.

S19932-4 Corydoras serratus   BROADBAND
W, 5 - 6cm
Venezuela: Rio Pina(north Maturin), Rio Amana + Tinaquilla.

S19932-4 Corydoras serratus   BROADBAND
W, 5 - 6cm
Venezuela: Rio Pina(north Maturin), Rio Amana + Tinaquilla.

S20429-4 Corydoras sp. C 29 "RONDONIA-LONGNOSE"
W, 5 - 6cm   DATZ 4/95
Brazil: Amapa

S20429-4 Corydoras sp. C 29 "RONDONIA-LONGNOSE"
W, 5 - 6cm   DATZ 4/95
Brazil: Amapa

S20432-4 Corydoras sp. C 32   DATZ 8/95
W, 5 - 6cm
Brazil: Rondonia

S18270-2 Corydoras cf. amapaensis sim.C.cortesi+ellisae JUVENIL
W, 5-6cm, Brazil: Cachoera Creek, branch to Rio Amapari, Aqua-
Branca Creek; Franz.Guyana: Maroni-river-system, Oyapock-system.

South America **all Corydoras**

S18270-4 Corydoras cf. amapaensis sim.C.cortesi+ellisae ADULT
W, 5-6cm, Brazil: Cachoera Creek, branch to Rio Amapari, Aqua-Branca Creek; Franz.Guyana: Maroni-river-system, Oyapock-system.

S18270-4 Corydoras cf. amapaensis sim.C.cortesi+ellisae JUVENIL
W, 5-6cm, Brazil: Cachoera Creek, branch to Rio Amapari, Aqua-Branca Creek; Franz.Guyana: Maroni-river-system, Oyapock-system.

S18730-4 Corydoras cortesi
W, 5 - 5,5cm
Peru: Provinz Loreto, Rio Huytoyacu by Nuevo Progresso.

S18730-4 Corydoras cortesi   PAIR
W, 5 - 5,5cm
Peru: Provinz Loreto, Rio Huytoyacu by Nuevo Progresso.

S18732-4 Corydoras sp. aff. cortesi (simulatus ?)
W, 5 - 5,5cm
Peru: Provinz Loreto, Rio Huytoyacu by Nuevo Progresso.

S18732-4 Corydoras sp. aff. cortesi (simulatus ?)   FEMALE
W, 5 - 5,5cm
Peru: Provinz Loreto, Rio Huytoyacu by Nuevo Progresso.

S18733-4 Corydoras cf. cortesi
W, 5 - 5,5cm
Peru: Provinz Loreto, Rio Huytoyacu by Nuevo Progresso.

S19565-4 Corydoras ourastigma
W, 6 - 7cm
Venezuela: San Fernando de Atabapo, Rio Atabapo+Orinoco c.tog.

S20130-4 CORYDORAS SP. FRANZ.GUIANA I griseus-longnose

S20130-4 CORYDORAS SP. FRANZ.GUIANA II griseus-longnose

South America **all Corydoras** 81

S19565-4 Corydoras ourastigma   MALE
W, 6 - 7cm
Venezuela: San Fernando de Atabapo, Rio Atabapo+Orinoco c.tog.

S19565-4 Corydoras ourastigma   FEMALE
W, 6 - 7cm
Venezuela: San Fernando de Atabapo, Rio Atabapo+Orinoco c.tog.

S19665-4 Corydoras pastazensis pastazensis
Synonym: pastacensis orcesi, W, 5 - 6cm
Brazil: Rio Negro - area, Rio Icana.

S19665-4 Corydoras pastazensis pastazensis
Synonym: pastacensis orcesi, W, 5 - 6cm
Brazil: Rio Negro - area, Rio Icana.

S19670-4 Corydoras pastazensis orcesi   similar C 32
Synonym: pastacensis orcesi, W, 5 - 6cm
Brazil: Rio Negro - area, Rio Icana.

S19668-4 Corydoras pastazensis orcesi   VARIANTE
Synonym: pastacensis orcesi, W, 5 - 6cm
Brazil: Rio Negro - area, Rio Icana.

S19850-4 Corydoras sarareensis "C 23"   MALE
W, 4 - 5cm
Surinam: Brokopondo-District, little Saramacca-river.

S19850-4 Corydoras sarareensis "C 23"   FEMALE
W, 4 - 5cm
Surinam: Brokopondo-District, little Saramacca-river.

South America **all Corydoras**   © Verlag A.C.S. GmbH

S19850-4 Corydoras sarareensis before C 23
W, 4 - 5cm
Surinam: Brokopondo-District, little Saramacca-river.

S19850-4 Corydoras sarareensis before C 23
W, 4 - 5cm
Surinam: Brokopondo-District, little Saramacca-river.

S20020-4 Corydoras solox
W, 6 - 7cm
Brazil: Rio Salimoes by Benjamin Constant; Peru: Loreto Rio Yavari.

S20050-4 Corydoras sp. "BRAZIL-LONGNOSE" similar C. ellisae
W, 5 - 6cm
Brazil

S20220-4 Corydoras sp. "MOTTLED" similar C. saraeensis MALE
W, 4 - 5cm
Surinam (?)

S20220-4 Corydoras sp. "MOTTLED" similar C. saraeensis FEMALE
W, 4 - 5cm
Surinam (?)

S20417-2 Corydoras sp. C 17 ("stenocephalus"?)   DATZ 4/94
W, 6 - 7cm
Bolivia (?)

S20438-4 Corydoras sp. C 38 similar C. serratus + C 29 "BRAZIL"
W, 5 - 6cm   DATZ 3/96
Brazil: Gojas

South America **all Corydoras**

S20820-4 Corydoras treitlii "BRAZIL" PAIR
W, 6 - 7cm
Brazil (?)

S20825-4 Corydoras cf. treitlii "PERU"
W, 6 - 7cm
Peru: Provinz Loreto, Rio Nanay, Rio Amazonas by Iquitos.

S20822-4 Corydoras sp. aff. treitlii adult
W, 6 - 7cm
Peru: Provinz Loreto, Rio Nanay, Rio Amazonas by Iquitos.

S20822-2 Corydoras sp. aff. treitlii juvenil
W, 6 - 7cm
Peru: Provinz Loreto, Rio Nanay, Rio Amazonas by Iquitos.

S19910-4 Corydoras septentrionalis
W, 4,5 - 5cm
Brazil: upper-branches to Rio Solimoes; Peru: Rio Ucayali-system.

S19910-4 Corydoras septentrionalis
W, 4,5 - 5cm
Brazil: upper-branches to Rio Solimoes; Peru: Rio Ucayali-system.

S19911-4 Corydoras septentrionalis VARIANTE I
W, 4,5 - 5cm
Brazil: upper-branches to Rio Solimoes; Peru: Rio Ucayali-system.

S19912-4 Corydoras septentrionalis VARIANTE II
W, 4,5 - 5cm
Brazil: upper-branches to Rio Solimoes; Peru: Rio Ucayali-system.

1. In solchen Zuchtteichen werden Corydoras gezüchtet.

In such breeding-ponds Corydoras are bred.

2. Zierfischfänger bei der Arbeit in Paraguay.

Ornamental-fish-catchers at work in Paraguay.

S19914-4 Corydoras intergrade septentrionalis / ellisae I
W, 4,5 - 5cm
Brazil: upper-branches to Rio Solimoes; Peru: Rio Ucayali-system.

S19913-4 Corydoras intergrade septentrionalis / ellisae II
W, 4,5 - 5cm
Brazil: upper-branches to Rio Solimoes; Peru: Rio Ucayali-system.

S19915-4 Corydoras intergrade septentrionalis / ellisae III
W, 4,5 - 5cm
Brazil: upper-branches to Rio Solimoes; Peru: Rio Ucayali-system.

S19916-4 Corydoras intergrade septentrionalis / ellisae IV
W, 4,5 - 5cm
Brazil: upper-branches to Rio Solimoes; Peru: Rio Ucayali-system.

S18850-4 Corydoras ellisae
W, 5 - 5,5cm
Paraguay, Sapucay, Arrogo Pona.

S18850-4 Corydoras ellisae
W, 5 - 5,5cm

S18851-4 Corydoras ellisae VARIANTE A PAIR
W, 5 - 5,5cm

S18852-4 Corydoras ellisae VARIANTE B
W, 5 - 5,5cm

South America all Corydoras

S18853-4 Corydoras ellisae VARIANTE C   PAIR
W, 5 - 5,5cm

S18853-2 Corydoras ellisae VARIANTE C   juvenil
W, 5 - 5,5cm

S18800-4 Corydoras ehrhardti   MALE
Synonym: meridionalis, W, 5 - 6cm
Brazil: Rio Poranga.

S18800-4 Corydoras ehrhardti   FEMALE
Synonym: meridionalis, W, 5 - 6cm
Brazil: Rio Poranga.

S18800-1 Corydoras ehrhardti
Synonym: meridionalis, W, 5 - 6cm
Brazil: Rio Poranga.

S18800-2 Corydoras ehrhardti
Synonym: meridionalis, W, 5 - 6cm
Brazil: Rio Poranga.

S18925-4 Corydoras flaveolus
W, 4,5 - 5cm
Surinam: Corantijn-area, Sisa-brook.

S18925-4 Corydoras flaveolus
W, 4,5 - 5cm
Surinam: Corantijn-area, Sisa-brook.

South America **all Corydoras**

S19200-4 Corydoras macropterus   MALE
Synonym: bertoni, W, 7 - 8cm
Columbia: Rio Ariari by Lomalinda.

S19200-4 Corydoras macropterus   FEMALE
Synonym: bertoni, W, 7 - 8cm
Columbia: Rio Ariari by Lomalinda.

S19200-4 Corydoras macropterus   MALE
Synonym: bertoni, W, 7 - 8cm
Columbia: Rio Ariari by Lomalinda.

S19200-4 Corydoras macropterus   FEMALE
Synonym: bertoni, W, 7 - 8cm
Columbia: Rio Ariari by Lomalinda.

S19585-4 Corydoras paleatus   MALE
Synonym: maculatus; marmoratus; microcephalus
W, 6 - 7cm, Surinam: Saramacca river-system, Goja-creek.

S19585-4 Corydoras paleatus   FEMALE
Synonym: maculatus; marmoratus; microcephalus
W, 6 - 7cm, Surinam: Saramacca river-system, Goja-creek.

S19586-4 Corydoras paleatus "FIN-SPOTTED"   PAIR
Synonym: maculatus; marmoratus; microcephalus
W, 6 - 7cm, Surinam: Saramacca river-system, Goja-creek.

S19586-4 Corydoras paleatus "FIN-SPOTTED"   FEMALE
Synonym: maculatus; marmoratus; microcephalus
W, 6 - 7cm, Surinam: Saramacca river-system, Goja-creek.

S19587-4 Corydoras paleatus "LARGE-SPOTTED" wild MALE
Synonym: maculatus; marmoratus; microcephalus
W, 6 - 7cm, Surinam: Saramacca river-system, Goja-creek.

S19587-4 Corydoras paleatus "LARGE-SPOTTED" wild FEMALE
Synonym: maculatus; marmoratus; microcephalus
W, 6 - 7cm, Argentina

S19588-4 Corydoras paleatus "HIGHFIN I" (cf. steindachneri)
W, 6 - 7cm
Argentina (?); Paraguay (?)

S19588-4 Corydoras paleatus "HIGHFIN I" (cf. steindachneri)
W, 6 - 7cm
Argentina (?); Paraguay (?)

S19589-4 Corydoras paleatus "HIGHFIN II" (cf. steindachneri)
W, 6 - 7cm   NATURFORM PAIR
Argentina (?); Paraguay (?)

S19589-4 Corydoras paleatus "HIGHFIN II" (cf. steindachneri)
W, 6 - 7cm   NATURFORM
Argentina (?); Paraguay (?)

S19590-4 Corydoras paleatus "HIGHFIN III" (cf. steindachneri)
W, 6 - 7cm   WILDFORM MALE
Argentina (?); Paraguay (?)

S19590-4 Corydoras paleatus "HIGHFIN III" (cf. steindachneri)
W, 6 - 7cm   WILDFORM PAIR
Argentina (?); Paraguay (?)

South America **all Corydoras**

S19595-4 Corydoras paleatus ALBINO MALE
B, 6 - 7cm

S19600-4 Corydoras paleatus GOLDEN
B, 6 - 7cm

S20090-4 Corydoras sp. aff. C 22 MALE DATZ 12/94
W, 5 - 6cm
Brazil: Rio-Xingu (Roraima?)

S20090-4 Corydoras sp. aff. C 22 FEMALE DATZ 12/94
W, 5 - 6cm
Brazil: Rio-Xingu (Roraima?)

S20090-4 Corydoras sp. aff. C 22 DATZ 12/94
W, 5 - 6cm
Brazil: Rio-Xingu (Roraima?)

S20735-4 Corydoras stenocephalus similar C. ellisae
W, 6 - 7cm
Brazil: Est. Parana, Paranaqua.

S18945-4 Corydoras garbei MALE
W, 4,5 - 5cm
Columbia: border to Peru; Peru: Loreto, Cano del Chancho by Pebas

S18945-4 Corydoras garbei FEMALE
W, 4,5 - 5cm
Columbia: border to Peru; Peru: Loreto, Cano del Chancho by Pebas

S19200-4 CORYDORAS MACROPTERUS

S20120-4 Corydoras sp. "FRANCISCO" very similar C. flaveoulus !
W, 4 - 5cm
Surinam (?); Paraguay (?)

S20407-2 Corydoras sp. C 07 very similar C.paleatus HIGHFIN I
W, 3,5 - 4cm   JUVENIL DATZ 12/93
Peru(?); Brazil; Bolivia: Beni, Rio-Tijamuchi/Rio-Marmore

S20407-4 Corydoras sp. C 07 very similar C.paleatus HIGHFIN I
W, 3,5 - 4cm   MALE DATZ 12/93
Peru(?); Brazil; Bolivia: Beni, Rio-Tijamuchi/Rio-Marmore

S20407-4 Corydoras sp. C 07 very similar C.paleatus HIGHFIN I
W, 3,5 - 4cm   FEMALE DATZ 12/93
Peru(?); Brazil; Bolivia: Beni, Rio-Tijamuchi/Rio-Marmore

S20422-4 Corydoras sp. C 22 very similar to sp.aff. C 22 MALE
W, 5 - 6cm   DATZ 12/94
Brazil: Roaima

S20422-4 Corydoras sp. C 22 very similar to sp.aff. C 22 FEMALE
W, 5 - 6cm   DATZ 12/94
Brazil: Roaima

S18575-2 Corydoras cf. aff. bifasciatus similar axelrodi JUVENIL
W, 4,5 - 5cm
Surinam: Corantijn-system, Sipalwini-river, Lucie-river.

S18575-4 Corydoras cf. aff. bifasciatus similar axelrodi
W, 4,5 - 5cm
Surinam: Corantijn-system, Sipalwini-river, Lucie-river.

S18565-4 Corydoras bondi bondi   MALE
W, 4,5 - 5cm   + Rio Yucuari
Guyana: Apaikwa; Surinam: Sipalwini; Venezuela: Edo Bolivar.

S18565-4 Corydoras bondi bondi   FEMALE
W, 4,5 - 5cm   + Rio Yucuari
Guyana: Apaikwa; Surinam: Sipalwini; Venezuela: Edo Bolivar.

S18565-4 Corydoras bondi bondi   PAIR
W, 4,5 - 5cm   + Rio Yucuari
Guyana: Apaikwa; Surinam: Sipalwini; Venezuela: Edo Bolivar.

S18567-4 Corydoras bondi coppenamensis   PAIR
W, 4 - 4,5cm
Surinam: Coppename-river, Sarramacca Creek.

S18567-4 Corydoras bondi coppenamensis   MALE
W, 4 - 4,5cm
Surinam: Coppename-river, Sarramacca Creek.

S18567-4 Corydoras bondi coppenamensis   FEMALE
W, 4 - 4,5cm
Surinam: Coppename-river, Sarramacca Creek.

S20431-4 Corydoras sp. C 31   similar C. bondi
W, 4 - 5cm   DATZ 8/95
Roraima/Brazil: upper-course of Rio-Branco,

S19430-4 Corydoras nattereri (before also C.juquiaae + triseriatus)
Synonym: juquiaae; nattereri triseriatus, W, 5-6cm PAIR
Brazil: Est. Amazonas, Rio Huaita.

South America **all Corydoras**

S19430-4 Corydoras nattereri   MALE
Synonym: juquiaae; nattereri triseriatus, W, 5 - 6cm
Brazil: Est. Amazonas, Rio Huaita.

S19430-4 Corydoras nattereri   FEMALE
Synonym: juquiaae; nattereri triseriatus, W, 5 - 6cm
Brazil: Est. Amazonas, Rio Huaita.

S19430-4 Corydoras nattereri
Synonym: juquiaae; nattereri triseriatus, W, 5 - 6cm
Brazil: Est. Amazonas, Rio Huaita.

S19433-4 Corydoras nattereri "SMALL-BAND"
Synonym: juquiaae; nattereri triseriatus, W, 5 - 6cm
Brazil: Est. Amazonas, Rio Huaita.

S19440-4 Corydoras sp. aff. nattereri   MALE
Synonym: juquiaae; nattereri triseriatus, W, 5 - 6cm
Brazil: Est. Amazonas, Rio Huaita.

S19440-4 Corydoras sp. aff. nattereri   FEMALE
Synonym: juquiaae; nattereri triseriatus, W, 5 - 6cm
Brazil: Est. Amazonas, Rio Huaita.

S19710-4 Corydoras prionotus MALE
Synonym: triseriatus, W, 5,5 - 6cm
Guyana: Essequibo, Potaro-river, brook by Potaro Landing.

S19710-4 Corydoras prionotus FEMALE
Synonym: triseriatus, W, 5,5 - 6cm
Guyana: Essequibo, Potaro-river, brook by Potaro Landing.

S18455-4 Corydoras axelrodi   MALE
W, 4,5 - 5cm
Columbia: Rio Meta by Vichada/Arauca + Boyaca.

S18455-4 Corydoras axelrodi   FEMALE
W, 4,5 - 5cm
Columbia: Rio Meta by Vichada/Arauca + Boyaca.

S18470-4 Corydoras axelrodi VARIANTE A MALE
W, 4,5 - 5cm
Columbia: Rio Meta by Vichada/Arauca + Boyaca.

S18470-4 Corydoras axelrodi VARIANTE A FEMALE
W, 4,5 - 5cm
Columbia: Rio Meta by Vichada/Arauca + Boyaca.

S18471-4 Corydoras axelrodi VARIANTE B PAIR
W, 4,5 - 5cm
Columbia: Rio Meta by Vichada/Arauca + Boyaca.

S18471-4 Corydoras axelrodi VARIANTE B
W, 4,5 - 5cm
Columbia: Rio Meta by Vichada/Arauca + Boyaca.

S18455-1 Corydoras axelrodi   JUVENIL 12 weeks old !
W, 4,5 - 5cm   (see DATZ 1/90 + 11/93 as C 03)
Columbia: Rio Meta by Vichada/Arauca + Boyaca.

S18471-1 Corydoras axelrodi VARIANTE B   SCHOOL juvenil
W, 4,5 - 5cm
Columbia: Rio Meta by Vichada/Arauca + Boyaca.

South America **all Corydoras**

S18665-4 Corydoras cf. cochui similar C 22
W, 2,5 - 3cm
Brazil: Est. Goias, Rio Araguaia by Santa Maria Nova.

S18665-4 Corydoras cf. cochui similar C 22
W, 2,5 - 3cm
Brazil: Est. Goias, Rio Araguaia by Santa Maria Nova.

S19190-4 Corydoras loxozonus
W, 4,5 - 5cm
Peru: Provinz Loreto, Rio Nanay.

S19190-2 Corydoras loxozonus similar C 20 JUVENIL
W, 4,5 - 5cm
Peru: Provinz Loreto, Rio Nanay.

S19020-4 Corydoras habrosus PAIR
W, 3 - 3,5cm
Surinam: Nickerie, Coppename + Saramacca - river-system.

S19022-4 Corydoras habrosus VARIANTE MALE
W, 3 - 3,5cm
Surinam: Nickerie, Coppename + Saramacca - river-system.

S19020-4 Corydoras habrosus MALE
W, 3 - 3,5cm
Surinam: Nickerie, Coppename + Saramacca - river-system.

S19020-4 Corydoras habrosus FEMALE
W, 3 - 3,5cm
Surinam: Nickerie, Coppename + Saramacca - river-system.

South America **all Corydoras**   © Verlag A.C.S. GmbH

S20408-4 Corydoras sp. C 08 "longnose to habrosus"!
W, 5 - 6cm   DATZ 12/93
Columbia

S18530-4 Corydoras barbatus   MALE
Synonym: eigenmanni; kronei. W, 10 - 12cm
Brazil: East-cost from Rio de Janeiro - Sao Paulo, central-highland.

S18530-4 Corydoras barbatus   MALE
Synonym: eigenmanni; kronei. W, 10 - 12cm
Brazil: East-cost from Rio de Janeiro - Sao Paulo, central-highland.

S18530-4 Corydoras barbatus   FEMALE
Synonym: eigenmanni; kronei. W, 10 - 12cm
Brazil: East-cost from Rio de Janeiro - Sao Paulo, central-highland.

S18530-4 Corydoras barbatus   Paarung / mating ! FEMALE
Synonym: eigenmanni; kronei. B, 10 - 12cm
Brazil: East-cost from Rio de Janeiro - Sao Paulo, central-highland.

S18530-4 Corydoras barbatus   Paarung / mating ! FEMALE
Synonym: eigenmanni; kronei. B, 10 - 12cm
Brazil: East-cost from Rio de Janeiro - Sao Paulo, central-highland.

S18530-4 Corydoras barbatus   Eier legendes Weibchen /
FEMALE egg-laying/oviparous !
Brazil: East-cost from Rio de Janeiro - Sao Paulo, central-highland.

S18530-1 Corydoras barbatus   baby, 5 weeks old !
Synonym: eigenmanni; kronei. B, 10 - 12cm
Brazil: East-cost from Rio de Janeiro - Sao Paulo, central-highland.

S18530-4 CORYDORAS BARBATUS (before also eigenmanni + kronei)

S18530-4 CORYDORAS BARBATUS (before also eigenmanni + kronei)

S18460-4 CORYDORAS AXELRODI mit Seitenstreifen / with side-stripe !   FEMALE

S18465-4 CORYDORAS AXELRODI ohne Seitenstreifen / without side-stripe !   MALE

South America **all Corydoras**

S20030-4 Corydoras sp. "BAIANINHO II" MALE
W, 5 - 6cm
Brazil

S20030-4 Corydoras sp. "BAIANINHO II" FEMALE
W, 5 - 6cm
Brazil

------------ Corydoras sp. "BAIANINHO II" GELEGE/spawn-hatching

S20030-1 Corydoras sp. "BAIANINHO II" baby, 8 weeks old !
B, 5 - 6cm
Brazil

S20270-4 Corydoras sp. "PERU-BLACK" (cf. semiaquilus)
W, 8 - 10cm
Peru

S20270-2 Corydoras sp. "PERU-BLACK" (cf. semiaquilus) JUVENIL
W, 8 - 10cm
Peru

S19105-4 Corydoras lacerdai (C 15) MALE
Synonym: "baianinho I" W, 4 -5cm
Brazil: Est. Maranhao, tributary to Rio Parnaiba.

S19105-4 Corydoras lacerdai (C 15) FEMALE
Synonym: "baianinho I" W, 4 -5cm
Brazil: Est. Maranhao, tributary to Rio Parnaiba.

South America all Corydoras © Verlag A.C.S. GmbH

S18810-4 Corydoras elegans   PAIR
          Synonym: pestai, W, 4,5 - 5cm
South-East-Brazil, into flowing off from the Jaraqua-mountains.

S18810-4 Corydoras elegans   FEMALE
          Synonym: pestai, W, 4,5 - 5cm
South-East-Brazil, into flowing off from the Jaraqua-mountains.

S18815-4 Corydoras elegans   VARIANTE I   MALE
          Synonym: pestai, W, 4,5 - 5cm
Brazil: by Tefe; Ecuador: Aguarico-system; Peru: Rio Napo-system.

S18815-4 Corydoras elegans   VARIANTE I   FEMALE
          Synonym: pestai, W, 4,5 - 5cm
Brazil: by Tefe; Ecuador: Aguarico-system; Peru: Rio Napo-system.

S18820-4 Corydoras elegans   VARIANTE II   MALE
          Synonym: pestai, W, 4,5 - 5cm
Brazil: by Tefe; Ecuador: Aguarico-system; Peru: Rio Napo-system.

S18820-4 Corydoras elegans   VARIANTE II   FEMALE
          Synonym: pestai, W, 4,5 - 5cm
Brazil: by Tefe; Ecuador: Aguarico-system; Peru: Rio Napo-system.

S18821-4 Corydoras elegans   VARIANTE III yellow   MALE
          Synonym: pestai, W, 4,5 - 5cm
Brazil: by Tefe; Ecuador: Aguarico-system; Peru: Rio Napo-system.

S18821-4 Corydoras elegans   VARIANTE III yellow   FEMALE
          Synonym: pestai, W, 4,5 - 5cm
Brazil: by Tefe; Ecuador: Aguarico-system; Peru: Rio Napo-system.

South America **all Corydoras**

S18822-4 Corydoras elegans VARIANTE IV MALE
Synonym: pestai, W, 4,5 - 5cm
Brazil: by Tefe; Ecuador: Aguarico-system; Peru: Rio Napo-system.

S18822-4 Corydoras elegans VARIANTE IV FEMALE
Synonym: pestai, W, 4,5 - 5cm
Brazil: by Tefe; Ecuador: Aguarico-system; Peru: Rio Napo-system.

S18822-4 Corydoras elegans VARIANTE IV FEMALE
Synonym: pestai, W, 4,5 - 5cm
Brazil: by Tefe; Ecuador: Aguarico-system; Peru: Rio Napo-system.

S18823-4 Corydoras elegans VARIANTE V PERU MALE
Synonym: pestai, W, 4,5 - 5cm
Brazil: by Tefe; Ecuador: Aguarico-system; Peru: Rio Napo-system.

S18824-4 Corydoras elegans VARIANTE VI MALE
Synonym: pestai, W, 4,5 - 5cm
Brazil: by Tefe; Ecuador: Aguarico-system; Peru: Rio Napo-system.

S18825-4 Corydoras elegans VARIANTE VII MALE
Synonym: pestai, W, 4,5 - 5cm
Brazil: by Tefe; Ecuador: Aguarico-system; Peru: Rio Napo-system.

S19120-4 Corydoras latus MALE
W, 4,5 - 5cm
Peru: Prov.Loreto, Rio Huytoyacu by Nuevo Progresso.

S19120-4 Corydoras latus FEMALE
W, 4,5 - 5cm
Peru: Prov.Loreto, Rio Huytoyacu by Nuevo Progresso.

S19120-4 Corydoras latus   MALE
W, 4,5 - 5cm
Peru: Prov.Loreto, Rio Huytoyacu by Nuevo Progresso.

S19120-1 Corydoras latus   BABY
B, 4,5 - 5cm
Peru: Prov.Loreto, Rio Huytoyacu by Nuevo Progresso.

S19395-4 Corydoras napoensis
W, 4,5 - 5cm   area of Gran Rio between Ligolio +
Surinam: Brokopondo-district,   the Awaram-waterfalls.

S19396-4 Corydoras napoensis VARIANTE I
W, 4,5 - 5cm   area of Gran Rio between Ligolio +
Surinam: Brokopondo-district,   the Awaram-waterfalls.

S19397-4 Corydoras napoensis VARIANTE II PAIR
W, 4,5 - 5cm   area of Gran Rio between Ligolio +
Surinam: Brokopondo-district,   the Awaram-waterfalls.

S19398-4 Corydoras napoensis VARIANTE III MALE
W, 4,5 - 5cm   area of Gran Rio between Ligolio +
Surinam: Brokopondo-district,   the Awaram-waterfalls.

S19755-4 Corydoras pygmaeus   PAIR
W, 2,5 - 3cm
Surinam: Rio Brokopondo, Oompagnie Creek; Guyana + Peru(?)

S19755-3 Corydoras pygmaeus   SCHWARM / SCHOOL
W, 2,5 - 3cm
Surinam: Rio Brokopondo, Oompagnie Creek; Guyana + Peru(?)

South America **all Corydoras**

S20190-4 Corydoras sp. HYBRIDE nijsseni x napoensis (?)
4 - 5cm
Brazil (?)

S20340-4 Corydoras sp. "SAN-JUAN" same as C. latus !
W, 4 - 5cm
Peru

S20441-4 Corydoras sp. C 41 similar C. elegans, but more dark !
W, 4 - 5cm   DATZ 3/96
Rondonia/Brazil,

S20900-4 Corydoras undulatus (before also C.microps) MALE
W, 4,5 - 5cm   also from Paraguay !!
Ecuador: Rio Pastaza; Peru: Rio Yavari,Huytoyacu,Yasuni,Nanay,

S20900-4 Corydoras undulatus MALE
W, 4,5 - 5cm   also from Paraguay !!
Ecuador: Rio Pastaza; Peru: Rio Yavari,Huytoyacu,Yasuni,Nanay,

S20900-4 Corydoras undulatus PAIR
W, 4,5 - 5cm   also from Paraguay !!
Ecuador: Rio Pastaza; Peru: Rio Yavari,Huytoyacu,Yasuni,Nanay,

S18050-4 Corydoras aeneus
W, 6 - 6,5cm   Venezuela: Rio Apure.
Bolivia; Brazil; Ecuador; Columbia; Peru; Surinam; Trinidad;

S18050-4 Corydoras aeneus
W, 6 - 6,5cm   Venezuela: Rio Apure.
Bolivia; Brazil; Ecuador; Columbia; Peru; Surinam; Trinidad;

S18080-4 Corydoras aeneus "BREEDING-FORM"
B, 5 - 6cm   Venezuela: Rio Apure.
Bolivia; Brazil; Ecuador; Columbia; Peru; Surinam; Trinidad;

S18105-4 Corydoras aeneus "BELEM" (before also macrosteus)
W, 6 - 6,5cm   Venezuela: Rio Apure.
Bolivia; Brazil; Ecuador; Columbia; Peru; Surinam; Trinidad;

S18135-4 Corydoras aeneus "PERU GREEN-STRIPE"
W, 6 - 6,5cm   Venezuela: Rio Apure.
Bolivia; Brazil; Ecuador; Columbia; Peru; Surinam; Trinidad;

S18145-4 Corydoras aeneus "PERU GOLD-STRIPE"
W, 6 - 6,5cm   Venezuela: Rio Apure.
Bolivia; Brazil; Ecuador; Columbia; Peru; Surinam; Trinidad;

S18145-4 Corydoras aeneus "PERU GOLD-STRIPE" PAIR
W, 6 - 6,5cm   Venezuela: Rio Apure.
Bolivia; Brazil; Ecuador; Columbia; Peru; Surinam; Trinidad;

S18145-4 Corydoras aeneus "PERU GOLD-STRIPE"
W, 6 - 6,5cm   Venezuela: Rio Apure.
Bolivia; Brazil; Ecuador; Columbia; Peru; Surinam; Trinidad;

S18095-4 Corydoras aeneus "PERU GOLD-SHOULDER RED"
W, 6 - 6,5cm   Venezuela: Rio Apure.
Bolivia; Brazil; Ecuador; Columbia; Peru; Surinam; Trinidad;

S18095-4 Corydoras aeneus "PERU GOLD-SHOULDER RED"
W, 6 - 6,5cm   Venezuela: Rio Apure.
Bolivia; Brazil; Ecuador; Columbia; Peru; Surinam; Trinidad;

South America **all Corydoras**

S18095-4 Corydoras aeneus "PERU GOLD-SHOULDER RED"
W, 6 - 6,5cm, "BLACK-HEAD"   Venezuela: Rio Apure.
Bolivia; Brazil; Ecuador; Columbia; Peru; Surinam; Trinidad;

S18065-4 Corydoras aeneus "GOLD-SHOULDER GREEN"
W, 6 - 6,5cm   Venezuela: Rio Apure.
Bolivia; Brazil; Ecuador; Columbia; Peru; Surinam; Trinidad;

S18150-4 Corydoras aeneus   VARIANTE dark I   MALE
W, 6 - 6,5cm   Venezuela: Rio Apure.
Bolivia; Brazil; Ecuador; Columbia; Peru; Surinam; Trinidad;

S18150-4 Corydoras aeneus   VARIANTE dark I   FEMALE
W, 6 - 6,5cm   Venezuela: Rio Apure.
Bolivia; Brazil; Ecuador; Columbia; Peru; Surinam; Trinidad;

S18155-4 Corydoras aeneus   VARIANTE dark II "RONDONIA"
W, 6 - 6,5cm   Venezuela: Rio Apure.
Bolivia; Brazil; Ecuador; Columbia; Peru; Surinam; Trinidad;

S18100-4 Corydoras aeneus   VARIANTE ohne Goldstreifen !
W, 6-6,5cm, without gold-stripes   Venezuela: Rio Apure.
Bolivia; Brazil; Ecuador; Columbia; Peru; Surinam; Trinidad;

S18070-4 Corydoras aeneus "BLACK"
W, 6 - 6,5cm   Venezuela: Rio Apure.
Bolivia; Brazil; Ecuador; Columbia; Peru; Surinam; Trinidad;

S18070-4 Corydoras aeneus "BLACK"
W, 6 - 6,5cm   Venezuela: Rio Apure.
Bolivia; Brazil; Ecuador; Columbia; Peru; Surinam; Trinidad;

S20270-4 CORYDORAS SP. "BLACK - PERU"

S18060-4 Corydoras aeneus "ALBINO"
B, 5 - 6cm

S18060-4 Corydoras aeneus "ALBINO"
B, 5 - 6cm

S18090-4 Corydoras aeneus "ALBINO" künstlich rotgespritzt ! /
B, 5 - 6cm   artificial red-injection !
-TIERQUÄLEREI / MISTREATMENT-

S18085-4 Corydoras aeneus   künstlich rotgespritzt /
B, 5 - 6cm   artificial red-injection !
-TIERQUÄLEREI / MISTREATMENT-

S18050-2 Corydoras aeneus JUVENIL
B, 5 - 6cm

S18160-4 Corydoras sp. aff. aeneus "VENEZUELA"
W, 6 - 6,5cm
Venezuela: Rio-Apure

S18160-4 Corydoras sp. aff. aeneus "VENEZUELA" MALE
W, 6 - 6,5cm
Venezuela: Rio Apure

S18160-4 Corydoras sp. aff. aeneus "VENEZUELA" FEMALE
W, 6 - 6,5cm
Venezuela: Rio Apure

---------- Corydoras sp. aff. aeneus "VENEZUELA"
Gelege/SPAWN

S18160-- Corydoras sp. aff. aeneus "VENEZUELA" baby,2 days old!
B, 5 - 6cm
Venezuela: Rio Apure

S18160-- Corydoras sp. aff. aeneus "VENEZUELA" baby,1 week old
B, 5 - 6cm
Venezuela: Rio Apure

S18160-1 Corydoras sp. aff. aeneus "VENEZUELA" (before myersi)
B, 5 - 6cm   baby, 3 weeks old!
Venezuela: Rio Apure

S18870-4 Corydoras eques
W, 4,5 - 5cm
Brazil: Est. Amapa, Cachoera Creek, Rio Amapari.

S18870-4 Corydoras eques
W, 4,5 - 5cm
Brazil: Est. Amapa, Cachoera Creek, Rio Amapari.

S18675-4 Corydoras concolor   MALE
W, 7 - 8cm
Brazil: Est. Gojas, Rio Araguaia by Santa Maria Nova.

S18675-4 Corydoras concolor   FEMALE
W, 7 - 8cm
Brazil: Est. Gojas, Rio Araguaia by Santa Maria Nova.

South America **all Corydoras**

S18675-4 Corydoras concolor   MALE
W, 7 - 8cm
Brazil: Est. Gojas, Rio Araguaia by Santa Maria Nova.

S18675-4 Corydoras concolor
W, 7 - 8cm
Brazil: Est. Gojas, Rio Araguaia by Santa Maria Nova.

S18675-1 Corydoras concolor   JUVENIL
W, 7 - 8cm
Brazil: Est. Gojas, Rio Araguaia by Santa Maria Nova.

S18680-4 Corydoras sp. aff. concolor
W, 7 - 8cm
Brazil: Est. Gojas, Rio Araguaia by Santa Maria Nova.

S19300-4 Corydoras melanotaenia   PAIR
W, 5,5 - 6cm
Guyana: Essequibo-river; Venezuela (?); Columbia !

S19300-4 Corydoras melanotaenia
W, 5,5 - 6cm
Guyana: Essequibo-river; Venezuela (?); Columbia !

S18550-3 Corydoras bolivianus   similar to C. sp. C 05   MALE
W, 5,5 - 6cm
Bolivia: Provinz Beni, Rio Mamore-basin.

S18550-3 Corydoras bolivianus   similar to C. sp. C 05   MALE
W, 5,5 - 6cm
Bolivia: Provinz Beni, Rio Mamore-basin.

S18555-4 Corydoras cf. bolivianus similar to C 05   MALE
W, 5,5 - 6cm
Bolivia: Provinz Beni, Rio Mamore-basin.

S18555-4 Corydoras cf. bolivianus similar to C 05   FEMALE
W, 5,5 - 6cm
Bolivia: Provinz Beni, Rio Mamore-basin.

S19765-4 Corydoras rabauti   PAIR
Synonym: myersi, W, 5,5 - 6cm
Brazil: Rondonia / Calama, Rio Madeira; Peru (?)

S19765-1 Corydoras rabauti   BABY - SCHOOL, 28 days old !
Synonym: myersi, B, 5,5 - 6cm

S19765-4 Corydoras rabauti
Synonym: myersi, W, 5,5 - 6cm
Brazil: Rondonia / Calama, Rio Madeira; Peru (?)

S19765-4 Corydoras rabauti
Synonym: myersi, W, 5,5 - 6cm
Brazil: Rondonia / Calama, Rio Madeira; Peru (?)

S19766-4 Corydoras rabauti   VARIANTE A (before C. myersi)
Synonym: myersi, W, 5,5 - 6cm
Brazil: Rondonia / Calama, Rio Madeira; Peru (?)

S19767-4 Corydoras rabauti   VARIANTE B
Synonym: myersi, W, 5,5 - 6cm
Brazil: Rondonia / Calama, Rio Madeira; Peru (?)

South America **all Corydoras**

S20405-4 Corydoras sp. C 05   MALE in Pracht / full colour !
Synonym: latus, W, 9 - 10cm   DATZ 12/93
Brazil: Mato-Grosso

S20405-4 Corydoras sp. C 05   MALE in Pracht / full colour !
Synonym: latus, W, 9 - 10cm   DATZ 12/93
Brazil: Mato-Grosso

S20405-3 Corydoras sp. C 05   MALE beginnende Umfärbung !
Synonym: latus, W, 9 - 10cm   DATZ 12/95
Brazil: Mato-Grosso   begining of colour-changing !

S20405-3 Corydoras sp. C 05   MALE beginnende Umfärbung !
Synonym: latus, W, 9 - 10cm   DATZ 12/93
Brazil: Mato-Grosso   begining of colour-changing !

S20405-3 Corydoras sp. C 05   MALE fortgeschrittene Umfärbung!
Synonym: latus, W, 9 - 10cm   DATZ 12/93
Brazil: Mato-Grosso   advanced colour-changing !

S20405-4 Corydoras sp. C 05   MALE Umfärbung abgeschlossen !
Synonym: latus, W, 9 - 10cm   DATZ 12/93
Brazil: Mato-Grosso   colour-changing ready !

S20405-4 Corydoras sp. C 05   FEMALE
Synonym: latus, W, 9 - 10cm   DATZ 12/93
Brazil: Mato-Grosso

S20405-4 Corydoras sp. C 05   FEMALE
Synonym: latus, W, 9 - 10cm   DATZ 12/93
Brazil: Mato-Grosso

S21050-4 Corydoras zygatus PAIR
W, 6 - 7cm
Brazil: Mato Grosso, Rio Xingu, Suia Missu Creek.

S21050-4 Corydoras zygatus PAIR
W, 6 - 7cm
Brazil: Mato Grosso, Rio Xingu, Suia Missu Creek.

S21050-4 Corydoras zygatus MALE
W, 6 - 7cm
Brazil: Mato Grosso, Rio Xingu, Suia Missu Creek.

S21050-4 Corydoras zygatus FEMALE
W, 6 - 7cm
Brazil: Mato Grosso, Rio Xingu, Suia Missu Creek.

S18980-4 Corydoras gossei MALE
W, 5 - 5,5cm
Columbia: Amazonas by Leticia, Isla de Mocaqua.

S18980-4 Corydoras gossei FEMALE
W, 5 - 5,5cm
Columbia: Amazonas by Leticia, Isla de Mocaqua.

S18980-4 Corydoras gossei FEMALE
W, 5 - 5,5cm
Columbia: Amazonas by Leticia, Isla de Mocaqua.

S18980-1 Corydoras gossei JUVENIL 4 weeks old !
B, 5 - 5,5cm
Columbia: Amazonas by Leticia, Isla de Mocaqua.

South America **all Corydoras**

S20405-4 CORYDORAS SP. C 05

S19040-3 CORYDORAS HASTATUS "SCHWARM / SCHOOL"

S19765-2 CORYDORAS RABAUTI JUVENIL "SCHWARM / SCHOOL"

S19955-4 Corydoras seussi (C 27)   ADULT
Synonym: "gossei longnose", W, 8 - 9cm, tributary to
Brazil: Rio Poranga, 8km north at Nobua oba,   upper Rio Negro.

S19955-4 Corydoras seussi (C 27)   PAIR
Synonym: "gossei longnose", W, 8 - 9cm   tributary to
Brazil: Rio Poranga, 8km north at Nobua oba,   upper Rio Negro.

S19955-2 Corydoras seussi (C 27)   SEMIADULT
Synonym: "gossei longnose", W, 8 - 9cm   tributary to
Brazil: Rio Poranga, 8km north at Nobua oba,   upper Rio Negro.

S19955-1 Corydoras seussi (C 27)   JUVENIL
Synonym: "gossei longnose", W, 8 - 9cm   tributary to
Brazil: Rio Poranga, 8km north at Nobua oba,   upper Rio Negro.

S18640-2 Corydoras caudimaculatus   SEMIADULT
W, 5,5 - 6cm
Brazil: Est. Rondonia, upper-course of Rio Guapore.

S18640-4 Corydoras caudimaculatus   ADULT
W, 5,5 - 6cm
Brazil: Est. Rondonia, upper-course of Rio Guapore.

S19010-4 Corydoras guapore
W, 4,5 - 5cm
Brazil: Est. Rondonia, upper-course of Rio Guapore.

S19010-4 Corydoras guapore
W, 4,5 - 5cm
Brazil: Est. Rondonia, upper-course of Rio Guapore.

S19010-4 Corydoras guapore
W, 4,5 - 5cm
Brazil: Est. Rondonia, upper-course of Rio Guapore.

S19010-4 Corydoras guapore
W, 4,5 - 5cm
Brazil: Est. Rondonia, upper-course of Rio Guapore.

S19040-3 Corydoras hastatus
W, 2,5 - 3cm
Brazil: Mato Grosso + Paraguay.

S19040-3 Corydoras hastatus
W, 2,5 - 3cm
Brazil: Mato Grosso + Paraguay.

S19040-3 Corydoras hastatus   (before also C. australe!)
W, 2,5 - 3cm
Brazil: Mato Grosso + Paraguay.

S31120-4 Dianema longibarbis (SCHWIELENWELS)
Synonym: Callichthys adspersus; Decapogon adspersu. W, 9-10cm
Rio Ambyiac (Peru) + Rio Pacaya.

S31130-4 Dianema urostriata
Synonym: Decapogon urostriatum, W, M. 9cm+ F. 12cm
Brazil: Rio Negro / Manaus-area.

S31135-4 Dianema cf. urostriata VARIANTE
Synonym: Decapogon urostriatum, W, M. 9cm+ F. 12cm
Brazil: Rio Negro / Manaus-area.

South America **all Corydoras**

S31120-4 DIANEMA LONGIBARBIS

S31130-4 DIANEMA UROSTRIATA

S11105-4 Callichthys callichthys (SCHWIELENWELS)
Syn.: Callichthys coelatus,laeviceps,loricatus; Silurus callichthys
W, 15-18cm, Brazil, Peru, Bolivia, Paraguay, Guyana, Venezuela.

S11108-2 Callichthys callichthys "MATO-GROSSO" semiadult
Syn.: Callichthys coelatus,laeviceps,loricatus; Silurus callichthys
W, 15-18cm, Brazil, Peru, Bolivia, Paraguay, Guyana, Venezuela.

S39020-2 Hoplosternum littorale (Synonym: Callichthys littoralis)
W, 20 - 22cm
mostly in whole Southamerica + Central-America.

S39025-2 Hoplosternum littorale "MATO-GROSSO" semiadult
W, 18 - 20cm
Paraguay,

S39030-2 Hoplosternum littorale "VENEZUELA" juvenil
W, 13 - 15cm
central-course of Orinoco, near Caicara

S39040-3 Hoplosternum pectorale
Syn.:Hoplost.magdalensis,pectoralis; Callichthys pectoralis
W, 11 - 13cm, Brazil: Rio Magdalena.

S39040-3 Hoplosternum pectorale
Syn.:Hoplost.magdalensis,pectoralis; Callichthys pectoralis
W, 11 - 13cm, Brazil: Rio Magdalena.

S39041-3 Hoplosternum cf. pectorale "DWARF"
- same as Hoplosternum sp. VII -
W, 8 - 9cm

South America **all Corydoras**

S39070-1 Hoplosternum cf. thoracatum   JUVENIL
W, 15 - 18cm
Brazil; Peru; Guyana; Venezuela; Paraguay; mostly in flat branches.

S39070-2 Hoplosternum cf. thoracatum
W, 15 - 18cm
Brazil; Peru; Guyana; Venezuela; Paraguay; mostly in flat branches.

S39070-2 Hoplosternum cf. thoracatum
W, 15 - 18cm
Brazil; Peru; Guyana; Venezuela; Paraguay; mostly in flat branches.

S39070-4 Hoplosternum cf. thoracatum   ADULT
W, 15 - 18cm
Brazil; Peru; Guyana; Venezuela; Paraguay; mostly in flat branches.

S39071-3 Hoplosternum sp. aff. thoracatum (magdalensis)
W, 15 - 18cm
Brazil; Peru; Guyana; Venezuela; Paraguay; mostly in flat branches.

S39071-3 Hoplosternum sp. aff. thoracatum (magdalensis)
W, 15 - 18cm
Brazil; Peru; Guyana; Venezuela; Paraguay; mostly in flat branches.

S39045-2 Hoplosternum sp. I (Hoplost. cf. thoracatum) juvenil
all Hoplosternum, Dianema+Callichthys are Schaumnestbauer /
W, 16-18cm, mostly whole Southamerica. bubble-nest-builder

S39045-4 Hoplosternum sp. I (Hoplost. cf. thoracatum) FEMALE
all Hoplosternum, Dianema+Callichthys are Schaumnestbauer /
W, 16-18cm, mostly whole Southamerica. bubble-nest-builder

South America all Corydoras   © Verlag A.C.S. GmbH

S39046-4 Hoplosternum sp. II (H. cf.thoracatum) MALE adult
Schaumnestbauer / bubble-nest-builder
W, 18 - 22cm, mostly whole Southamerica.

S39046-4 Hoplosternum sp. II (H. cf.thoracatum) FEMALE
Schaumnestbauer / bubble-nest-builder
W, 18 - 22cm, mostly whole Southamerica.

S39046-4 Hoplosternum sp. II (H. cf.thoracatum) MALE
in Laichfärbung / spawning-colour !
W, 18 - 22cm, mostly whole Southamerica.

S39046-1 Hoplosternum sp. II (H. cf.thoracatum) JUVENIL
Schaumnestbauer / bubble-nest-builder
W, 18 - 22cm, mostly whole Southamerica.

S39047-4 Hoplosternum sp. III (H. cf. orinocoi)) MALE adult
Schaumnestbauer / bubble-nest-builder
W, 14 - 16cm, mostly whole Southamerica.

S39047-4 Hoplosternum sp. III (H. cf. orinocoi) FEMALE adult
Schaumnestbauer / bubble-nest-builder
W, 14 - 16cm, mostly whole Southamerica.

S39048-4 Hoplosternum sp. IV (H. cf.thoracatum) similar Dianema
Schaumnestbauer / bubble-nest-builder
B, 8 - 9cm, mostly whole Southamerica.

S39048-4 Hoplosternum sp. IV (H. cf.thoracatum) similar Dianema
Schaumnestbauer / bubble-nest-builder
B, 8 - 9cm, mostly whole Southamerica.

S39048-4 Hoplosternum sp. IV (H. cf. lithorale) MALE
Schaumnestbauer / bubble-nest-builder
B, 8 - 9cm, mostly whole Southamerica.

S39048-4 Hoplosternum sp. IV (H. cf. lithorale) FEMALE
Schaumnestbauer / bubble-nest-builder
B, 8 - 9cm, mostly whole Southamerica.

S39049-3 Hoplosternum sp. V same as H.cf.pectorale "DWARF"
W, 8 - 9cm
origin unknown !

S39050-3 Hoplosternum sp. VI LONG-BEART" (H.cf.pectorale)
W, 9 - 10cm
origin unknown !

L 014a Scobiancistrus aureatus "GOLDY - PLECO"
Den + alle anderen finden Sie / these + all other you will find
in "LORICARIIDAE all L - Numbers" !

Crenicichla sp. "XINGU III"
Den + alle anderen finden Sie / these + all other you will find
in "SOUTHAMERICAN CICHLIDS I" !

Geophagus sp. altifrons "RIO NEGRO"
Den + alle anderen finden Sie / these + all other you will find
in "SOUTHAMERICAN CICHLIDS I" !

Apistogramma hongsloi II
Den + alle anderen finden Sie / these + all other you will find
in "SOUTHAMERICAN CICHLIDS II" !

Lieber Leser,

Sollten Sie im Besitz kleiner oder großer Dia- oder Foto-Sammlungen sein, bitte setzen Sie sich mit uns in Verbindung. Wir suchen für unsere nächsten Bücher immer gute Bilder von allen Fisch-Arten und besonders schönen Aquarien, und würden Ihre Bilder, natürlich gegen eine angemessene Benutzungsgebühr, gerne veröffentlichen.

To our readers,

if you are in possession of either a small or large collection of slides or photographs please contact us. For our upcoming books we are always on the lookout for good pictures of all types of fish and also for attractive aquariums. We would like to publish your photographs - obviously for a suitable charge.

In regelmäßigen Abständen erscheinen Ergänzungen mit neuen Fisch-Bildern, die können Sie

hier

einkleben, damit Sie immer "up-to-date" sind.

Supplements featuring new fish-photographs will be issued on regular basis. Stick them in

here

so that your collection is always up to date.

In regelmäßigen Abständen erscheinen Ergänzungen mit neuen Fisch-Bildern, die können Sie

hier

einkleben, damit Sie immer "up-to-date" sind.

Supplements featuring new fish-photographs will be issued on regular basis. Stick them in

here

so that your collection is always up to date.

In regelmäßigen Abständen erscheinen Ergänzungen mit neuen Fisch-Bildern, die können Sie

Supplements featuring new fish-photographs will be issued on regular basis. Stick them in

In regelmäßigen Abständen erscheinen Ergänzungen mit neuen Fisch-Bildern, die können Sie

hier

einkleben, damit Sie immer "up-to-date" sind.

Supplements featuring new fish-photographs will be issued on regular basis. Stick them in

here

so that your collection is always up to date.

In regelmäßigen Abständen erscheinen Ergänzungen mit neuen Fisch-Bildern, die können Sie

hier

einkleben, damit Sie immer "up-to-date" sind.

Supplements featuring new fish-photographs will be issued on regular basis. Stick them in

here

so that your collection is always up to date.

In regelmäßigen Abständen erscheinen Ergänzungen mit neuen Fisch-Bildern, die können Sie

hier

einkleben, damit Sie immer "up-to-date" sind.

Supplements featuring new fish-photographs will be issued on regular basis. Stick them in

here

so that your collection is always up to date.

South America **all Corydoras** © Verlag A.C.S. GmbH

INDEX
Code - numbers

Code	Name	Page
S05115	Aspidoras lakoi	17
S06102	Aspidoras albater	17
S06105	Aspidoras brunneus	9
S06108	Aspidoras carvalhoi	9
S06110	Aspidoras cf. eurycephalus	17
S06112	Aspidoras fuscoguttatus	9
S06118	Aspidoras maculosus	9
S06119	Aspidoras cf. maculosus	17
S06121	Aspidoras menezesi	18
S06123	Aspidoras pauciradiatus	18
S06126	Aspidoras cf. poecilius	18
S06130	Aspidoras raimundi	9
S06135	Aspidoras rochai	9
S06140	Aspidoras sp. "ARAGUAIA"	18
S06145	Aspidoras sp. "BLACK-PHANTOM" (C35)	18,19
S06150	Aspidoras sp. "GOIA" (C37)	19
S06165	Aspidoras virgulatus	9
S09105	Brochis britskii	19
S09110	Brochis multiradiatus	19
S09120	Brochis splendens	20
S09123	Brochis splendens "SPOTTED"	20
S09125	Brochis splendens "BLACK"	20
S11105	Callichthys callichthys	119
S11108	Callichthys callichthys "MATO - GROSSO"	119
S18010	Corydoras acrensis	10
S18015	Corydoras acutus	20
S18025	Corydoras adolfoi	69,73,74
S18035	Corydoras adolfoi "VARIANTE SPOTTED"	74
S18040	Corydoras adolfoi HYBRIDE	73
S18041	Corydoras adolfoi HYBRIDE	73
S18050	Corydoras aeneus	104,108
S18060	Corydoras aeneus "ALBINO"	108
S18065	Corydoras aeneus "PERU GOLD - SHOULDER GREEN"	106
S18070	Corydoras aeneus "BLACK"	106
S18080	Corydoras aeneus "BREEDING - FORM"	105
S18090	Corydoras aeneus "ALBINO" rotgespritzt !	108
S18095	Corydoras aeneus "PERU GOLD - SHOULDER RED"	105,106
S18100	Corydoras aeneus "VARIANTE WITHOUT GOLD - STRIPES"	106
S18105	Corydoras aeneus "BELEM"	105
S18135	Corydoras aeneus "PERU GREEN - STRIPE"	105
S18145	Corydoras aeneus "PERU GOLD - STRIPE"	105
S18150	Corydoras aeneus "VARIANTE DARK I"	106
S18155	Corydoras aeneus "VARIANTE DARK II RONDONIA"	106
S18160	Corydoras sp. aff. aeneus "VENEZUELA"	108,109
S18200	Corydoras agassizii	27
S18205	Corydoras agassizii "VARIANTE"	28
S18210	Corydoras sp. aff. agassizii	28
S18230	Corydoras amandajanea similar C. cryticus + burgessi	67
S18245	Corydoras sp. aff. amandajanea	67
S18265	Corydoras amapaensis	10
S18270	Corydoras cf. amapaensis similar C. cortesi + elisae	79,80
S18285	Corydoras ambiacus	28
S18288	Corydoras ambiacus "VARIANTE"	28
S18289	Corydoras ambiacus "VARIANTE"	28
S18295	Corydoras sp. aff. ambiacus	31
S18298	Corydoras cf. ambiacus "PERU"	28
S18300	Corydoras amphibelus	10
S18310	Corydoras approuaguensis	10
S18320	Corydoras araguaiaensis	46,48
S18325	Corydoras araguaiaensis "VARIANTE I"	48
S18326	Corydoras araguaiaensis "VARIANTE II"	48
S18355	Corydoras arcuatus	64,67,68
S18365	Corydoras sp. aff. arcuatus "BROKEN - STRIPE"	68
S18375	Corydoras arcuatus "SUPER - ARCUATUS" same as C. 20	27,68
S18395	Corydoras armatus	31
S18398	Corydoras cf. armatus	31
S18405	Corydoras atropersonatus	22
S18415	Corydoras atropersonatus "VARIANTE I"	22
S18418	Corydoras atropersonatus "VARIANTE II"	22,34
S18419	Corydoras atropersonatus "VARIANTE III"	22
S18425	Corydoras aurofrenatus	10
S18455	Corydoras axelrodi	95
S18460	Corydoras axelrodi with side - stripe	99
S18470	Corydoras axelrodi "VARIANTE A"	95
S18471	Corydoras axelrodi "VARIANTE B"	95
S18515	Corydoras sp. aff. blochi vittatus	23
S18515	Corydoras baderi	10
S18530	Corydoras barbatus	97,98
S18530	Corydoras boehlkei	10

INDEX
Code - numbers

Code	Name	Page
S18540	Corydoras boesemani	11
S18550	Corydoras bolivianus similar to C. sp. C 05	110
S18555	Corydoras cf. bolivianus	111
S18565	Corydoras bondi bondi	93
S18567	Corydoras bondi coppenamensis	93
S18568	Corydoras HYBRIDE bondi coppenamensis + surinamensis	13
S18575	Corydoras cf. aff. bifasciatus similar axelrodi	92
S18576	Corydoras bifasciatus	10
S18585	Corydoras sp. aff. blochi blochi	23
S18585	Corydoras breei	62
S18590	Corydoras cf. blochi blochi	22
S18595	Corydoras cf. blochi blochi	22
S18600	Corydoras blochi vittatus	21,23
S18600	Corydoras burgessi	68,69,71
S18602	Corydoras burgessi "VARIANTE SPOTTED" BREEDING-FORM	71
S18604	Corydoras burgessi "VARIANTE SPOTTED"	71
S18605	Corydoras burgessi "VARIANTE STRIPED"	71
S18615	Corydoras sp. aff. burgessi	71
S18630	Corydoras carlae	11
S18640	Corydoras caudimaculatus	116
S18650	Corydoras cervinus	58
S18652	Corydoras cervinus "HELL/ LIGHT A"	58
S18665	Corydoras cf. cochui similar C 22	96
S18675	Corydoras concolor	109,11
S18680	Corydoras sp. aff. concolor	110
S18690	Corydoras condiscipulus	54,63
S18691	Corydoras condiscipulus "COLOUR - VARIANTE A"	63
S18692	Corydoras condiscipulus "COLOUR - VARIANTE B"	63
S18693	Corydoras condiscipulus "COLOUR - VARIANTE C"	63
S18705	Corydoras copei	11
S18730	Corydoras cortesi	80
S18732	Corydoras sp. aff. cortesi	80
S18733	Corydoras cf. cortesi	80
S18745	Corydoras crypticus	72
S18746	Corydoras crypticus HYBRIDE (?)	72
S18747	Corydoras crypticus "SPOTTED"	72
S18755	Corydoras davidsandsi	70,77
S18765	Corydoras delphax	32
S18770	Corydoras sp. aff. delphax	32
S18775	Corydoras cf. delphax	32
S18775	Corydoras sp. aff. crypticus	72
S18790	Corydoras duplicareus	74
S18800	Corydoras ehrhardti	87
S18810	Corydoras elegans	101
S18815	Corydoras elegans "VARIANTE I"	101
S18820	Corydoras elegans "VARIANTE II"	101
S18821	Corydoras elegans "VARIANTE III"	101
S18822	Corydoras elegans "VARIANTE IV"	102
S18823	Corydoras elegans "VARIANTE V"	102
S18824	Corydoras elegans "VARIANTE VI"	102
S18825	Corydoras elegans "VARIANTE VII"	102
S18850	Corydoras ellisae	86
S18851	Corydoras ellisae "VARIANTE A"	86
S18852	Corydoras ellisae "VARIANTE B"	86
S18853	Corydoras ellisae "VARIANTE C"	87
S18860	Corydoras ephippifer	11
S18870	Corydoras eques	109
S18885	Corydoras esperanzae	11
S18900	Corydoras evelynae	23
S18903	Corydoras evelynae "VARIANTE"	23
S18906	Corydoras evelynae "VARIANTE I"	23,26
S18920	Corydoras filamentosus	11
S18925	Corydoras flaveolus	87
S18935	Corydoras fowleri	11
S18945	Corydoras garbei	90
S18960	Corydoras sp. aff. geryi same as C 11	48,52
S18970	Corydoras gomezi	48
S18980	Corydoras gossei	113
S18995	Corydoras gracilis	11
S19000	Corydoras griseus "echt/ true" very similar to C 40	63
S19005	Corydoras cf. griseus very similar to C 40	66
S19010	Corydoras guapore	116,117
S19015	Corydoras guiaensis	12
S19020	Corydoras habrosus	96
S19022	Corydoras habrosus "VARIANTE"	96
S19030	Corydoras haraldschultzi	48,49
S19040	Corydoras hastatus	115,117
S19045	Corydoras heteromorphus	12
S19055	Corydoras imitator	74

INDEX
Code - numbers

Code	Name	Page
S19080	Corydoras incolicana (before C 01)	32,33,38
S19085	Corydoras incolicana "VARIANTE I" (C 01)	33,38
S19086	Corydoras incolicana "VARIANTE II" (C 01)	33,38
S19088	Corydoras sp. aff. incolicana	33
S19095	Corydoras julii	49
S19098	Corydoras julii "VARIANTE I"	49
S19099	Corydoras julii "VARIANTE II"	49
S19105	Corydoras lacerdai (C 15)	100
S19110	Corydoras lamberti	12
S19120	Corydoras latus	102,103
S19135	Corydoras leopardus	49
S19138	Corydoras leopardus "VARIANTE"	49
S19150	Corydoras leucomelas (before C. caquetae)	33
S19155	Corydoras leucomelas "VARIANTE"	35
S19160	Corydoras cf. leucomelas	35
S19165	Corydoras leucomelas "VARIANTE PERU"	33
S19175	Corydoras loretoensis	62,63
S19190	Corydoras loxozonus	96
S19200	Corydoras macropterus	88,91
S19210	Corydoras maculifer	51
S19250	Corydoras melanistius ssp. intergrade I	36
S19251	Corydoras melanistius ssp. intergrade II	36
S19260	Corydoras melanistius brevirostris (before C. wotroi)	24,36
S19265	Corydoras melanistius brevirostris "VARIANTE"	37
S19270	Corydoras melanistius melanistius	35
S19275	Corydoras melanistius melanistius "VARIANTE"	35
S19280	Corydoras cf. melanistius melanistius	35,36
S19281	Coridoras cf. melanistius melanistius "SURINAM"	36
S19290	Corydoras cf. ambiacus "SPOTTED II"	28
S19300	Corydoras melanotaenia	110
S19315	Corydoras melini	77
S19340	Corydoras metae	70,77
S19342	Corydoras metae "VARIANTE"	77
S19360	Corydoras micracanthus	12
S19370	Corydoras cf. multimaculatus	37
S19375	Corydoras sp. aff. multimaculatus	37
S19385	Corydoras nanus	12
S19395	Corydoras napoensis	103
S19396	Corydoras napoensis "VARIANTE I"	103
S19397	Corydoras napoensis "VARIANTE II"	103
S19398	Corydoras napoensis "VARIANTE III"	103
S19410	Corydoras narcissus	65,76
S19430	Corydoras nattereri (before also C. juquiaae + triseriatus)	93,94
S19433	Corydoras nattereri "SMALL - BAND"	94
S19440	Corydoras sp. aff. nattereri	94
S19450	Corydoras nijsseni	69,75
S19452	Corydoras nijsseni "VARIANTE SPOTTED"	75
S19454	Corydoras nijsseni "VARIANTE BROADBAND"	75
S19455	Corydoras nijsseni "VARIANTE BLACK"	76
S19470	Corydoras sp. aff. nijsseni "LONGNOSE"	76
S19500	Corydoras octocirrhus	12
S19510	Corydoras oiapoquensis	66
S19511	Corydoras oiapoquensis "VARIANTE A"	66
S19512	Corydoras oiapoquensis "VARIANTE B"	66
S19513	Corydoras oiapoquensis "VARIANTE C"	66
S19514	Corydoras oiapoquensis "VARIANTE D"	66
S19515	Corydoras sp. aff. oiapoquensis "PLANE - TAIL"	67
S19530	Corydoras ornatus "WHITE - TOP"	43
S19531	Corydoras ornatus	12
S19535	Corydoras cf. ornatus	43
S19537	Corydoras sp. aff. ornatus	43
S19545	Corydoras orphnopterus	12
S19555	Corydoras osteocarus	51
S19565	Corydoras ourastigma	80,82
S19575	Corydoras oxyrhynchus	13
S19585	Corydoras paleatus	88
S19586	Corydoras paleatus "FIN - SPOTTED"	88
S19587	Corydoras paleatus "LARGE - SPOTTED"	89
S19588	Corydoras paleatus "HIGHFIN I" (cf. steindachneri)	89
S19589	Corydoras paleatus "HIGHFIN II" (cf. steindachneri)	89
S19590	Corydoras paleatus "HIGHFIN III" (cf. steindachneri)	89
S19595	Corydoras paleatus "ALBINO"	90
S19600	Corydoras paleatus "GOLDEN"	90
S19630	Corydoras panda "BIG - SPOT"	78
S19635	Corydoras panda "SMALL - SPOT"	78
S19650	Corydoras parallelus "C 02"	25,37,38
S19665	Corydoras pastazensis pastazensis	82
S19668	Corydoras pastazensis orcesi "VARIANTE"	82
S19670	Corydoras pastazensis orcesi similar C 32	82

INDEX
Code - numbers

Code	Species	Page
S19680	Corydoras pinheiroi (C 25)	51,52
S19690	Corydoras polystictus	60
S19692	Corydoras polystictus "XANTHORIST/ YELLOW"	60
S19695	Corydoras polystictus "VARIANTE"	60
S19700	Corydoras cf. potaroensis	67
S19710	Corydoras prionotus	94
S19720	Corydoras pulcher	50
S19722	Corydoras pulcher "VARIANTE I"	43,44
S19723	Corydoras pulcher "VARIANTE II"	44
S19724	Corydoras pulcher "VARIANTE III"	44
S19735	Corydoras punctatus	13
S19755	Corydoras pygmaeus	103
S19765	Corydoras rabauti	111,115
S19766	Corydoras rabauti "VARIANTE A"	111
S19767	Corydoras rabauti "VARIANTE B"	111
S19775	Corydoras reticulatus	56,59
S19778	Corydoras reticulatus "VARIANTE"	56
S19800	Corydoras reynoldsi	13
S19810	Corydoras robineae	42,51,52
S19820	Corydoras robustus	44
S19830	Corydoras sanchesi	13
S19840	Corydoras cf. saramaccensis	26
S19841	Corydoras saramaccensis	13
S19850	Corydoras sarareensis "C 23"	82,83
S19860	Corydoras schwartzi	44,45,50
S19862	Corydoras schwartzi "VARIANTE I"	45
S19863	Corydoras schwartzi "VARIANTE II"	45
S19865	Corydoras schwartzi "VARIANTE III"	45
S19866	Corydoras schwartzi "VARIANTE IV" very simil C.pulcher	45
S19867	Corydoras schwartzi "VARIANTE V"	45
S19868	Corydoras schwartzi "VARIANTE VI"	45
S19910	Corydoras septentrionalis	84
S19911	Corydoras septentrionalis "VARIANTE I"	84
S19912	Corydoras septentrionalis "VARIANTE II"	84
S19913	Corydoras intergrade septentrionalis / ellisae II	86
S19914	Corydoras intergrade septentrionalis / ellisae I	86
S19915	Corydoras intergrade septentrionalis / ellisae III	86
S19916	Corydoras intergrade septentrionalis / ellisae IV	86
S19932	Corydoras serratus "BROADBAND"	79
S19935	Corydoras serratus same as C 29	79
S19953	Corydoras cervinus "HELL/ LIGHT B"	58
S19955	Corydoras seussi (C 27)	116
S19970	Corydoras similis	60
S19980	Corydoras simulatus	78
S19983	Corydoras simulatus "VARIANTE"	78
S20000	Corydoras sodalis	57,59
S20003	Corydoras sodalis "HOCHRÜCKEN/ HIGH - BODY"	57
S20004	Corydoras sodalis "GESTRECKT/ LOW - BODY"	57
S20005	Corydoras sodalis "VARIANTE GREY"	57
S20008	Corydoras sodalis "ROUND - HEAD"	57
S20020	Corydoras solox	83
S20030	Corydoras sp. "BAIANINHO II"	100
S20040	Corydoras sp. "BRAZIL" simil. C.schwartzi "VARIANTE III"	45
S20050	Corydoras sp. "BRAZIL - LONGNOSE" similar C. ellisae	83
S20060	Corydoras sp. "BRAZIL-RONDONIA"	26
S20070	Corydoras sp. "BRAZIL - SHARPHEAD"	52
S20080	Corydoras sp. "CORREA" (same as C 02 parallelus)	37
S20090	Corydoras sp. aff. C 22	90
S20110	Corydoras sp. "FALSO - ROBUSTUS"	46
S20120	Corydoras sp. "FRANCISCO" very similar C. flaveoulus	92
S20130	Corydoras sp. "FRANZ: - GUIANA I"	81
S20150	Corydoras sp. "GOLD"	61
S20160	Corydoras sp. HYBRIDE	72
S20170	Corydoras sp. HYBRIDE	72
S20180	Corydoras sp. HYBRIDE	72
S20190	Corydoras sp. HYBRIDE nijsseni x napoensis	104
S20200	Corydoras sp. HYBRIDE	72
S20210	Corydoras sp.HYBRIDE (panda x oiapoquensis)	30
S20220	Corydoras sp. "MOTTLED" similar C. saraeensis	83
S20230	Corydoras sp. "PERREIRA"	38
S20250	Corydoras sp. "PERU"	46
S20260	Corydoras sp. "PERU I"	52
S20270	Corydoras sp. "PERU - BLACK"	100,107
S20290	Corydoras sp. "RIO NEGRO I"	46
S20300	Corydoras sp. "RIO NEGRO II"	38
S20310	Corydoras sp "RIO TAPAJOS"	38
S20320	Corydoras cf. sanchesi very similar C 14	63
S20330	Corydoras sp. "RONDONIA" similar C 33 (R 8 in Japan)	38
S20340	Corydoras sp. "SAN - JUAN" same as C. latus	102,103,104

INDEX
Code - numbers

Code	Name	Page
S20360	Corydoras sp. "SPOTTED - LINE"	46
S20370	Corydoras sp. "SPOTTED - LONGNOSE"	38
S20380	Corydoras sp. "THREE - SPOTT - LINES"	46
S20401	Corydoras sp. C 01 same /now C. incolicana	33,38
S20402	Corydoras sp. C 02 same/now C. parallelus	37,38
S20403	Corydoras sp. C03 ("deckeri")	26
S20405	Corydoras sp. C 05	112,114
S20406	Corydoras sp. C 06 very similar to C. melan. brevirostris	38
S20407	Corydoras sp. C 07 very similar C paleatus "HIGHFIN I"	92
S20408	Corydoras sp. C 08 "longnose to C. habrosus"	97
S20409	Corydoras sp. C 09	40
S20410	Corydoras sp. C 10 similar C. agassizii	40
S20411	Corydoras sp. C 11 same/now C.sp. aff. geryi	48,52
S20412	Corydoras sp. C 12	52
S20413	Corydoras sp. C 13	52
S20414	Corydoras sp. C 14 similar C. sanchesi	61
S20415	Corydoras sp. aff. C 14 ("RIO BRANCO")	61
S20416	Corydoras sp. C 16	78
S20417	Corydoras sp. C 17 ("stenocephalus"?)	83
S20418	Corydoras sp. C 18 similar C. julii, leopardus, trillineatus	40
S20419	Corydoras sp. C19	26
S20420	Corydoras sp. C20 "VARIANTE"	27,68
S20421	Corydoras sp. C 21	40
S20422	Corydoras sp. C 22 very similar to sp. aff. C 22	92
S20424	Corydoras sp. C 24 similar C. servinus	58
S20426	Corydoras sp. C26	27
S20428	Corydoras sp. C 28 similar C. servinus + blochi	58
S20429	Corydoras sp. C 29 "RONDONIA - LONGNOSE"	79
S20430	Corydoras sp. C 30 similar to C. melanistius brevirostris	40
S20431	Corydoras sp. C 31 similar C. bondi	93
S20432	Corydoras sp. C 32	79
S20433	Corydoras sp. C 33 "VARIANTE"	40
S20434	Corydoras sp. C 34 same/similar C. sp. "RED - CHEEK"	41
S20438	Corydoras sp. C 38	83
S20439	Corydoras sp. C 39 similar C.davidsandsi, but longnose	76
S20440	Corydoras sp. C 40 very similar C. cf. griseus "RONDONIA"	67
S20441	Corydoras sp. C 41 similar C. elegans, but more dark	104
S20442	Corydoras sp. C 42 ("KRISTINAE") very similar C 24	58
S20443	Corydoras sp. C 43	41
S20444	Corydoras sp. C 44	41
S20445	Corydoras sp. C 45 same C. cf. araguaiaensis "BIG-SPOT"	56
S20446	Corydoras sp. C 46 similar C. sp. "RIO BRANCO"	41
S20700	Corydoras spilurus	13
S20735	Corydoras stenocephalus	90
S20750	Corydoras sterbai	53
S20760	Corydoras surinamensis	39,41
S20770	Corydoras cf. surinamensis	41,43
S20800	Corydoras sychri	27,34
S20820	Corydoras treitlii "BRAZIL"	84
S20822	Corydoras sp. aff. treitlii	84
S20825	Corydoras cf. treitlii "PERU"	84
S20840	Corydoras trilineatus	47,56
S20845	Corydoras trilineatus "VARIANTE"	56
S20900	Corydoras undulatus (before also C. microps)	104
S20940	Corydoras virginiae C 04	73
S20942	Corydoras virginiae C 04 "VARIANTE"	73
S20950	Corydoras virginiae C 04 "VARIANTE, HYBRIDE"	73
S20970	Corydoras weitzmani	13
S21000	Corydoras xinguensis	61
S21003	Corydoras xinguensis "VARIANTE A"	61
S21004	Corydoras xinguensis "VARIANTE B"	62
S21050	Corydoras zygatus	113
S31120	Dianema longibarbis	117,118
S31130	Dianema urostriata	117,118
S31135	Dianema cf. urostriata	117
S39020	Hoplosternum littorale (Synonym Callichthys littoralis)	119
S39025	Hoplosternum littorale "MATO - GROSSO"	119
S39030	Hoplosternum littorale "VENEZUELA"	119
S39040	Hoplosternum pectorale	119
S39041	Hoplosternum cf. pectorale "DWARF"	119
S39045	Hoplosternum sp I (H. cf. thoracatum)	120
S39046	Hoplosternum sp. II (H. cf. thoracatum)	121
S39047	Hoplosternum sp. III (H. cf. orinocoi)	121
S39048	Hoplosternum sp. IV (H. cf. thoracatum)	121,122
S39049	Hoplosternum sp. V same as H. cf. pectorale "DWARF"	122
S39070	Hoplosternum cf. thoracatum	120
S39071	Hoplosternum sp. aff. thoracatum (magdalensis)	120

INDEX
Alphabet

acrensis, Corydoras	10
acutus, Corydoras	20
adolfoi, Corydoras	69,73,74
aeneus, Corydoras	104,108
agassizzi, Corydoras	27
albater, Aspidoras	17
amandajanea, Corydoras	67
amapaensis, Corydoras	10
ambiacus, Corydoras	28
amphibelus, Corydoras	10
approuaguensis, Corydoras	10
araguaiaensis, Corydoras	46,48
arcuatus, Corydoras	64,67,68
armatus, Corydoras	31
Aspidoras albater	17
Aspidoras brunneus	9
Aspidoras carvalhoi	9
Aspidoras cf. eurycephalus	17
Aspidoras cf. maculosus	17
Aspidoras cf.poecilius	18
Aspidoras fuscoguttatus	9
Aspidoras lakoi	17
Aspidoras maculosus	9
Aspidoras menezesi	18
Aspidoras pauciradiatus	18
Aspidoras raimundi	9
Aspidoras rochai	9
Aspidoras sp. "ARAGUAIA"	18
Aspidoras sp. "BLACK-PHANTOM" (C35)	18,19
Aspidoras sp. "GOIA" (C37)	19
Aspidoras virgulatus	9
atropersonatus, Corydoras	22
aurofrenatus, Corydoras	10
axelrodi, Corydoras	95
baderi, Corydoras	10
barbatus, Corydoras	97,98
bertoni, Corydoras	88,91
bifasciatus, Corydoras	10
boehlkei, Corydoras	10
boesemani, Corydoras	11
bolivianus, Corydoras	110
bondi bondi, Corydoras	93
bondi coppenamensis, Corydoras	93
breei, Corydoras	62
brevirostris melanistius, Corydoras	24,36
britskii, Brochis	19
Brochis britskii	19
Brochis multiradiatus	19
Brochis splendens	20
Brochis splendens "BLACK"	20
Brochis splendens "SPOTTED"	20
brunneus, Aspidoras	9
burgessi, Corydoras	68,69,71
C 01 now incolicana Corydoras	32,33,38
C 01 sp., Corydoras	33,38
C 02 parallelus, Corydoras	25,37,38
C 02 sp., Corydoras	37,38
C 03 ("deckeri") sp., Corydoras	26
C 04 virginiae, Corydoras	73
C 05 sp., Corydoras	112,114
C 06 sp., Corydoras	38
C 07 sp., Corydoras	92
C 08 sp., Corydoras	97
C 09 sp., Corydoras	40
C 10 sp., Corydoras	40
C 11 sp., Corydoras	48,52
C 12 sp., Corydoras	52
C 13 sp., Corydoras	52
C 14 sp., Corydoras	61
C 15 lacerdai, Corydoras	100
C 16 sp., Corydoras	78
C 17 sp., Corydoras	83
C 18 sp., Corydoras	40
C 19 sp., Corydoras	26
C 20 "VARIANTE" sp., Corydoras	27,68
C 20 arcuatus "SUPER - ARCUATUS", Corydoras	27,68
C 21 sp., Corydoras	40
C 22 sp. aff., Corydoras	90
C 22 sp., Corydoras	92
C 23 sarareensis, Corydoras	82,83
C 24 sp., Corydoras	58
C 25 pinheiroi, Corydoras	51,52
C 26 sp., Corydoras	27
C 27 seussi, Corydoras	116
C 28 sp., Corydoras	58
C 29 "RONDONIA - LONGNOSE" sp., Corydoras	79
C 30 sp., Corydoras	40
C 31 sp., Corydoras	93
C 32 sp., Corydoras	79
C 33 sp. "VARIANTE", Corydoras	40
C 34 sp., Corydoras	41
C 35 "BLACK-PHANTOM" sp., Aspidoras	18,19
C 37 "GOIA" sp., Aspidoras	19
C 38 sp., Corydoras	83
C 39 sp., Corydoras	76
C 40 sp., Corydoras	67
C 41 sp., Corydoras	104
C 42 sp., Corydoras	58
C 43 sp., Corydoras	41
C 44 sp., Corydoras	41
C 45 sp., Corydoras	56
C 46 sp., Corydoras	41
Callichthys callichthys	119
Callichthys callichthys "MATO - GROSSO"	119
caquetae, Corydoras	33
carlae, Corydoras	11
carvalhoi, Aspidoras	9
caudimaculatus, Corydoras	116
cervinus, Corydoras	58
cf. "PERU" ambiacus, Corydoras	28
cf. "SPOTTED II" ambiacus, Corydoras	28
cf. aff. bifasciatus, Corydoras	92
cf. armatus, Corydoras	31
cf. blochi blochi, Corydoras	22
cf. bolivianus, Corydoras	111
cf. cochui, Corydoras	96
cf. cortesi, Corydoras	80
cf. delphax, Corydoras	32
cf. eurycephalus, Aspidoras	17
cf. griseus, Corydoras	66
cf. leucomelas, Corydoras	35
cf. makulosus, Aspidoras	17
cf. melanistius melanistius, Corydoras	35,36
cf. multimaculatus, Corydoras	37
cf. ornatus, Corydoras	43
cf. pectorale "DWARF", Hoplosternum	119
cf. poecilius, Aspidoras	18
cf. potaroensis, Corydoras	67
cf. sanchesi, Corydoras	63
cf. saramaccensis, Corydoras	26
cf. surinamensis, Corydoras	41,43
cf. thoracatum, Hoplosternum	120
cf. treitlii "PERU", Corydoras	84
cf. urostriata, Dianema	117
cf.amapaensis, Corydoras	79,80
concolor, Corydoras	109,110
condiscipulus, Corydoras	54,63
copei, Corydoras	11
Coridoras cf. melanistius melanistius "SURINAM"	36
cortesi, Corydoras	80
Corydoras acrensis	10
Corydoras acutus	20
Corydoras adolfoi	69,73,74
Corydoras adolfoi "VARIANTE SPOTTED"	74
Corydoras adolfoi HYBRIDE	73
Corydoras adolfoi HYBRIDE	73
Corydoras aeneus	104,108
Corydoras aeneus "ALBINO"	108
Corydoras aeneus "ALBINO" rotgespritzt !	108
Corydoras aeneus "BELEM"	105
Corydoras aeneus "BLACK"	106
Corydoras aeneus "BREEDING - FORM"	105
Corydoras aeneus "PERU GOLD - SHOULDER GREEN"	106
Corydoras aeneus "PERU GOLD - SHOULDER RED"	105,106
Corydoras aeneus "PERU GOLD - STRIPE"	105
Corydoras aeneus "PERU GREEN - STRIPE"	105
Corydoras aeneus "VARIANTE DARK I"	106
Corydoras aeneus "VARIANTE DARK II RONDONIA"	106

INDEX
Alphabet

Corydoras aeneus "VARIANTE WITHOUT GOLD-STRIPES"	106
Corydoras agassizii	27
Corydoras agassizii "VARIANTE"	28
Corydoras amandajanea similar C. crypticus + burgessi	67
Corydoras amapaensis	10
Corydoras ambiacus	28
Corydoras ambiacus "VARIANTE"	28
Corydoras ambiacus "VARIANTE"	28
Corydoras amphibelus	10
Corydoras approuaguensis	10
Corydoras araguaiaensis	46,48
Corydoras araguaiaensis "VARIANTE I"	48
Corydoras araguaiaensis "VARIANTE II"	48
Corydoras arcuatus	64,67,68
Corydoras arcuatus "SUPER-ARCUATUS" same as C. 20	27,68
Corydoras armatus	31
Corydoras atropersonatus	22
Corydoras atropersonatus "VARIANTE I"	22
Corydoras atropersonatus "VARIANTE II"	22,34
Corydoras atropersonatus "VARIANTE III"	22
Corydoras aurofrenatus	10
Corydoras axelrodi	95
Corydoras axelrodi "VARIANTE A"	95
Corydoras axelrodi "VARIANTE B"	95
Corydoras axelrodi with side-stripe	99
Corydoras baderi	10
Corydoras barbatus	97,98
Corydoras bertoni	88,91
Corydoras bifasciatus	10
Corydoras blochi vittatus	21,23
Corydoras boehlkei	10
Corydoras boesemani	11
Corydoras bolivianus similar to C. sp. C 05	110
Corydoras bondi bondi	93
Corydoras bondi coppenamensis	93
Corydoras breei	62
Corydoras burgessi	68,69,71
Corydoras burgessi "VARIANTE SPOTTED"	71
Corydoras burgessi "VARIANTE SPOTTED" BREEDING-FORM	71
Corydoras burgessi "VARIANTE STRIPED"	71
Corydoras caquetae	33
Corydoras carlae	11
Corydoras caudimaculatus	116
Corydoras cervinus	58
Corydoras cervinus "HELL/LIGHT A"	58
Corydoras cervinus "HELL/LIGHT B"	58
Corydoras cf. aff. bifasciatus similar axelrodi	92
Corydoras cf. amapaensis similar C. cortesi + elisae	79,80
Corydoras cf. ambiacus "PERU"	28
Corydoras cf. ambiacus "SPOTTED II"	28
Corydoras cf. armatus	31
Corydoras cf. blochi blochi	22
Corydoras cf. blochi blochi	22
Corydoras cf. bolivianus	111
Corydoras cf. cochui similar C 22	96
Corydoras cf. cortesi	80
Corydoras cf. delphax	32
Corydoras cf. griseus very similar to C 40	66
Corydoras cf. leucomelas	35
Corydoras cf. melanistius melanistius	35,36
Corydoras cf. multimaculatus	37
Corydoras cf. ornatus	43
Corydoras cf. potaroensis	67
Corydoras cf. sanchesi very similar C 14	63
Corydoras cf. saramaccensis	26
Corydoras cf. surinamensis	41,43
Corydoras cf. treitlii "PERU"	84
Corydoras concolor	109,110
Corydoras condiscipulus	54,63
Corydoras condiscipulus "COLOUR-VARIANTE A"	63
Corydoras condiscipulus "COLOUR-VARIANTE B"	63
Corydoras condiscipulus "COLOUR-VARIANTE C"	63
Corydoras copei	11
Corydoras cortesi	80
Corydoras crypticus	72
Corydoras crypticus "SPOTTED"	72
Corydoras crypticus HYBRIDE (?)	72
Corydoras davidsandsi	70,77
Corydoras delphax	32
Corydoras dubius	47,56
Corydoras duplicareus	74
Corydoras ehrhardti	87
Corydoras eigenmanni	97,98
Corydoras elegans	101
Corydoras elegans "VARIANTE I"	101
Corydoras elegans "VARIANTE II"	101
Corydoras elegans "VARIANTE III"	101
Corydoras elegans "VARIANTE IV"	102
Corydoras elegans "VARIANTE V"	102
Corydoras elegans "VARIANTE VI"	102
Corydoras elegans "VARIANTE VII"	102
Corydoras elegans nijsseni	69,75
Corydoras ellisae	86
Corydoras ellisae "VARIANTE A"	86
Corydoras ellisae "VARIANTE B"	86
Corydoras ellisae "VARIANTE C"	87
Corydoras ephippifer	11
Corydoras episcopi	47,56
Corydoras eques	109
Corydoras esperanzae	11
Corydoras evelynae	23
Corydoras evelynae "VARIANTE I"	23,26
Corydoras evelynae "VARIANTE"	23
Corydoras filamentosus	11
Corydoras flaveolus	87
Corydoras fowleri	11
Corydoras funnelli	49
Corydoras garbei	90
Corydoras gomezi	48
Corydoras gossei	113
Corydoras gracilis	11
Corydoras grafi	28
Corydoras griseus "echt/true" very similar to C 40	63
Corydoras griseus deweyeri	63
Corydoras guapore	116,117
Corydoras guiaensis	12
Corydoras habrosus	96
Corydoras habrosus "VARIANTE"	96
Corydoras haraldschultzi	48,49
Corydoras hastatus	115,117
Corydoras heteromorphus	12
Corydoras HYBRIDE bondi coppenamensis + surinamensis	13
Corydoras imitator	74
Corydoras incolicana "VARIANTE I" (C 01)	33,38
Corydoras incolicana "VARIANTE II" (C 01)	33,38
Corydoras incolicana (before C 01)	32,33,38
Corydoras intergrade septentrionalis / ellisae I	86
Corydoras intergrade septentrionalis / ellisae II	86
Corydoras intergrade septentrionalis / ellisae III	86
Corydoras intergrade septentrionalis / ellisae IV	86
Corydoras julii	49
Corydoras julii "VARIANTE I"	49
Corydoras julii "VARIANTE II"	49
Corydoras juquiaae	93,94
Corydoras kronei	97,98
Corydoras lacerdai (C 15)	100
Corydoras lamberti	12
Corydoras latus	102,103
Corydoras leopardus	49
Corydoras leopardus "VARIANTE"	49
Corydoras leucomelas "VARIANTE PERU"	33
Corydoras leucomelas "VARIANTE"	35
Corydoras leucomelas (before C. caquetae)	33
Corydoras loretoensis	62,63
Corydoras loxozonus	96
Corydoras macropterus	88,91
Corydoras macrosteus	104,108
Corydoras maculatus	88
Corydoras maculifer	51
Corydoras marmoratus	88
Corydoras melanistius brevirostris "VARIANTE"	37
Corydoras melanistius brevirostris (before C. wotroi)	24,36
Corydoras melanistius longirostris	28
Corydoras melanistius melanistius	35
Corydoras melanistius melanistius "VARIANTE"	35
Corydoras melanistius ssp. intergrade I	36
Corydoras melanistius ssp. intergrade II	36
Corydoras melanotaenia	110

INDEX
Alphabet

Corydoras melini	77
Corydoras meridionalis	87
Corydoras metae	70,77
Corydoras metae "VARIANTE"	77
Corydoras micracanthus	12
Corydoras microcephalus	88
Corydoras microps	104
Corydoras myersi	111,115
Corydoras nanus	12
Corydoras napoensis	103
Corydoras napoensis "VARIANTE I"	103
Corydoras napoensis "VARIANTE II"	103
Corydoras napoensis "VARIANTE III"	103
Corydoras narcissus	65,76
Corydoras nattereri "SMALL - BAND"	94
Corydoras nattereri (before also C. juquiaae + triseriatus)	93,94
Corydoras nattereri triseriatus	93,94
Corydoras nijsseni	69,75
Corydoras nijsseni "VARIANTE BLACK"	76
Corydoras nijsseni "VARIANTE BROADBAND"	75
Corydoras nijsseni "VARIANTE SPOTTED"	75
Corydoras octocirrhus	12
Corydoras oelemariensis	10
Corydoras oiapoquensis	66
Corydoras oiapoquensis "VARIANTE A"	66
Corydoras oiapoquensis "VARIANTE B"	66
Corydoras oiapoquensis "VARIANTE C"	66
Corydoras oiapoquensis "VARIANTE D"	66
Corydoras ornatus	12
Corydoras ornatus "WHITE - TOP"	43
Corydoras orphnopterus	12
Corydoras osteocarus	51
Corydoras ourastigma	80,82
Corydoras oxyrhynchus	13
Corydoras paleatus	88
Corydoras paleatus "ALBINO"	90
Corydoras paleatus "FIN - SPOTTED"	88
Corydoras paleatus "GOLDEN"	90
Corydoras paleatus "HIGHFIN I" (cf. steindachneri)	89
Corydoras paleatus "HIGHFIN II" (cf. steindachneri)	89
Corydoras paleatus "HIGHFIN III" (cf. steindachneri)	89
Corydoras paleatus "LARGE - SPOTTED"	89
Corydoras panda "BIG - SPOT"	78
Corydoras panda "SMALL - SPOT"	78
Corydoras parallelus "C 02"	25,37,38
Corydoras pastazensis orcesi "VARIANTE"	82
Corydoras pastazensis orcesi similar C 32	82
Corydoras pastazensis pastazensis	82
Corydoras pestai	101
Corydoras pinheiroi (C 25)	51,52
Corydoras polystictus	60
Corydoras polystictus "VARIANTE"	60
Corydoras polystictus "XANTHORIST/ YELLOW"	60
Corydoras prionotus	94
Corydoras pulcher	50
Corydoras pulcher "VARIANTE I"	43,44
Corydoras pulcher "VARIANTE II"	44
Corydoras pulcher "VARIANTE III"	44
Corydoras punctatus	13
Corydoras pygmaeus	103
Corydoras rabauti	111,115
Corydoras rabauti "VARIANTE A"	111
Corydoras rabauti "VARIANTE B"	111
Corydoras reticulatus	56,59
Corydoras reticulatus "VARIANTE"	56
Corydoras reynoldsi	13
Corydoras robineae	42,51,52
Corydoras robustus	44
Corydoras sanchesi	13
Corydoras saramaccensis	13
Corydoras sarareensis "C 23"	82,83
Corydoras schultzei	104,108
Corydoras schwartzi	44,45,50
Corydoras schwartzi "VARIANTE I"	45
Corydoras schwartzi "VARIANTE II"	45
Corydoras schwartzi "VARIANTE III"	45
Corydoras schwartzi "VARIANTE IV" very simil C.pulcher	45
Corydoras schwartzi "VARIANTE V"	45
Corydoras schwartzi "VARIANTE VI"	45
Corydoras septentrionalis	84
Corydoras septentrionalis "VARIANTE I"	84
Corydoras septentrionalis "VARIANTE II"	84
Corydoras serratus "BROADBAND"	79
Corydoras serratus same as C 29	79
Corydoras seussi (C 27)	116
Corydoras similis	60
Corydoras simulatus	78
Corydoras simulatus "VARIANTE"	78
Corydoras sodalis	57,59
Corydoras sodalis "GESTRECKT/ LOW - BODY"	57
Corydoras sodalis "HOCHRÜCKEN/ HIGH - BODY"	57
Corydoras sodalis "ROUND - HEAD"	57
Corydoras sodalis "VARIANTE GREY"	57
Corydoras solox	83
Corydoras sp "RIO TAPAJOS"	38
Corydoras sp. "BAIANINHO II"	100
Corydoras sp. "BRAZIL - LONGNOSE" similar C. ellisae	83
Corydoras sp. "BRAZIL - SHARPHEAD"	52
Corydoras sp. "BRAZIL" simil. C.schwartzi "VARIANTE III"	45
Corydoras sp. "BRAZIL-RONDONIA"	26
Corydoras sp. "CORREA" (same as C 02 parallelus)	37
Corydoras sp. "FALSO - ROBUSTUS"	46
Corydoras sp. "FRANCISCO" very similar C. flaveoulus	92
Corydoras sp. "FRANZ: - GUIANA I"	81
Corydoras sp. "GOLD"	61
Corydoras sp. "MOTTLED" similar C. saraeensis	83
Corydoras sp. "PERREIRA"	38
Corydoras sp. "PERU - BLACK"	100,107
Corydoras sp. "PERU I"	52
Corydoras sp. "PERU"	46
Corydoras sp. "RIO NEGRO I"	46
Corydoras sp. "RIO NEGRO II"	38
Corydoras sp. "RONDONIA" similar C 33 (R 8 in Japan)	38
Corydoras sp. "SAN - JUAN" same as C. latus	102,103,104
Corydoras sp. "SPOTTED - LINE"	46
Corydoras sp. "SPOTTED - LONGNOSE"	38
Corydoras sp. "THREE - SPOTT - LINES"	46
Corydoras sp. aff. aeneus "VENEZUELA"	108,109
Corydoras sp. aff. agassizii	28
Corydoras sp. aff. amandajanea	67
Corydoras sp. aff. ambiacus	31
Corydoras sp. aff. arcuatus "BROKEN - STRIPE"	68
Corydoras sp. aff. blochi blochi	23
Corydoras sp. aff. blochi vittatus	23
Corydoras sp. aff. burgessi	71
Corydoras sp. aff. C 14 ("RIO BRANCO")	61
Corydoras sp. aff. C 22	90
Corydoras sp. aff. concolor	110
Corydoras sp. aff. cortesi	80
Corydoras sp. aff. crypticus	72
Corydoras sp. aff. delphax	32
Corydoras sp. aff. geryi same as C 11	48,52
Corydoras sp. aff. incolicana	33
Corydoras sp. aff. multimaculatus	37
Corydoras sp. aff. nattereri	94
Corydoras sp. aff. nijsseni "LONGNOSE"	76
Corydoras sp. aff. oiapoquensis "PLANE - TAIL"	67
Corydoras sp. aff. ornatus	43
Corydoras sp. aff. treitlii	84
Corydoras sp. C 01 same /now C. incolicana	33,38
Corydoras sp. C 02 same/now C. parallelus	37,38
Corydoras sp. C 05	112,114
Corydoras sp. C 06 very similar to C. melan. brevirostris	38
Corydoras sp. C 07 very similar C paleatus "HIGHFIN I"	92
Corydoras sp. C 08 "longnose to C. habrosus"	97
Corydoras sp. C 09	40
Corydoras sp. C 10 similar C. agassizii	40
Corydoras sp. C 11 same/now C.sp. aff. geryi	48,52
Corydoras sp. C 12	52
Corydoras sp. C 13	52
Corydoras sp. C 14 similar C. sanchesi	61
Corydoras sp. C 16	78
Corydoras sp. C 17 ("stenocephalus"?)	83
Corydoras sp. C 18 similar C. julii, leopardus, trillineatus	40
Corydoras sp. C 21	40
Corydoras sp. C 22 very similar to sp. aff. C 22	92
Corydoras sp. C 24 similar C. servinus	58
Corydoras sp. C 28 similar C. servinus + blochi	58

INDEX
Alphabet

Corydoras sp. C 29 "RONDONIA - LONGNOSE"	79
Corydoras sp. C 30 similar to C. melanistius brevirostris	40
Corydoras sp. C 31 similar C. bondi	93
Corydoras sp. C 32	79
Corydoras sp. C 33 "VARIANTE"	40
Corydoras sp. C 34 same/similar C. sp. "RED - CHEEK"	41
Corydoras sp. C 38	83
Corydoras sp. C 39 similar C.davidsandsi, but longnose	76
Corydoras sp. C 40 very similar C. cf. griseus "RONDONIA"	67
Corydoras sp. C 41 similar C. elegans, but more dark	104
Corydoras sp. C 42 ("KRISTINAE") very similar C 24	58
Corydoras sp. C 43	41
Corydoras sp. C 44	41
Corydoras sp. C 45 same C. cf. araguaiaensis "BIG-SPOT"	56
Corydoras sp. C 46 similar C. sp. "RIO BRANCO"	41
Corydoras sp. C03 ("deckeri")	26
Corydoras sp. C19	26
Corydoras sp. C20 "VARIANTE"	27,68
Corydoras sp. C26	27
Corydoras sp. HYBRIDE	72
Corydoras sp. HYBRIDE	72
Corydoras sp. HYBRIDE	72
Corydoras sp. HYBRIDE	72
Corydoras sp. HYBRIDE nijsseni x napoensis	104
Corydoras sp.HYBRIDE (panda x oiapoquensis)	30
Corydoras spilurus	13
Corydoras stenocephalus	90
Corydoras sterbai	53
Corydoras surinamensis	39,41
Corydoras sychri	27,34
Corydoras treitlii "BRAZIL"	84
Corydoras trilineatus	47,56
Corydoras trilineatus "VARIANTE"	56
Corydoras undulatus (before also C. microps)	104
Corydoras venezuelanus	104,108
Corydoras virescens	60
Corydoras virginiae C 04	73
Corydoras virginiae C 04 "VARIANTE"	73
Corydoras virginiae C 04 "VARIANTE, HYBRIDE"	73
Corydoras weitzmani	13
Corydoras wotroi	24,36
Corydoras xinguensis	61
Corydoras xinguensis "VARIANTE A"	61
Corydoras xinguensis "VARIANTE B"	62
Corydoras zygatus	113
crypticus, Corydoras	72
davidsandsi, Corydoras	70,77
delphax, Corydoras	32
deweyeri griseus, Corydoras	63
Dianema cf. urostriata	117
Dianema longibarbis	117,118
Dianema urostriata	117,118
dubius, Corydoras	47,56
duplicareus, Corydoras	74
eigenmanni, Corydoras	97,98
elegans, Corydoras	101
ellisae, Corydoras	86
ephippifer, Corydoras	11
episcopi, Corydoras	47,56
eques, Corydoras	109
erhardti, Corydoras	87
esperanzae, Corydoras	11
evelynae, Corydoras	23
filamentosus, Corydoras	11
flaveolus, Corydoras	87
fowleri, Corydoras	11
funnelli, Corydoras	49
fuscoguttatus, Aspidoras	9
garbei, Corydoras	90
gomezi, Corydoras	48
gossei, Corydoras	113
gracilis, Corydoras	11
grafi, Corydoras	28
griseus, Corydoras	63
guapore, Corydoras	116,117
guiaensis, Corydoras	12
habrosus, Corydoras	96
haraldschultzi, Corydoras	48,49
hastatus, Corydoras	115,117
heteromorphus, Corydoras	12
Hoplosternum cf. pectorale "DWARF"	119
Hoplosternum cf. thoracatum	120
Hoplosternum littorale "MATO - GROSSO"	119
Hoplosternum littorale "VENEZUELA"	119
Hoplosternum littorale (Synonym Callichthys littoralis)	119
Hoplosternum pectorale	119
Hoplosternum sp I (H. cf. thoracatum)	120
Hoplosternum sp. aff. thoracatum (magdalensis)	120
Hoplosternum sp. II (H. cf. thoracatum)	121
Hoplosternum sp. III (H. cf. orinocoi)	121
Hoplosternum sp. IV (H. cf. thoracatum)	121,122
Hoplosternum sp. V same as H. cf. pectorale "DWARF"	122
imitator, Corydoras	74
julii, Corydoras	49
juquiaae, Corydoras	93,94
kronei, Corydoras	97,98
lakoi, Aspidoras	17
lamberti, Corydoras	12
latus, Corydoras	102,103
leopardus, Corydoras	49
leucomelas, Corydoras (before C. caquetae)	33
littorale, Hoplosternum	119
longibarbis, Dianema	117,118
loretoensis, Corydoras	62,63
loxozonus, Corydoras	96
macropterus, Corydoras	88,91
macrosteus, Corydoras	104,108
maculatus, Corydoras	88
maculifer, Corydoras	51
maculosus, Aspidoras	9
marmoratus, Corydoras	88
melanistius longirostris, Corydoras	28
melanistius melanistius, Corydoras	35
melanotaenia, Corydoras	110
melini, Corydoras	77
menezesi, Aspidoras	18
meridionalis, Corydoras	87
metae, Corydoras	70,77
micracanthus, Corydoras	12
microcephalus, Corydoras	88
microps, Corydoras	104
multiradiatus, Brochis	19
myersi, Corydoras	111,115
nanus, Corydoras	12
napoensis, Corydoras	103
narcissus, Corydoras	65,76
nattereri, Corydoras	93,94
nattereri triseriatus, Corydoras	93,94
nijsseni elegans, Corydoras	69,75
nijsseni, Corydoras	69,75
octocirrhus, Corydoras	12
oelemariensis, Corydoras	10
oiapoquensis, Corydoras	66
ornatus "WHITE - TOP", Corydoras	43
ornatus, Corydoras	12
orphnopterus, Corydoras	12
ostocarus, Corydoras	51
ourastigma, Corydoras	80,82
oxyrhynchus, Corydoras	13
paleatus, Corydoras	88
panda "BIG - SPOT", Corydoras	78
pastazensis orcesi, Corydoras	82
pastazensis pastazensis, Corydoras	82
pauciradiatus, Aspidoras	18
pectorale, Hoplosternum	119
pestai, Corydoras	101
polystictus, Corydoras	60
prionotus, Corydoras	94
pulcher, Corydoras	50
pulcher, Corydoras	43,44
punctatus, Corydoras	13
pygmaeus, Corydoras	103
rabauti, Corydoras	111,115
raimundi, Aspidoras	9
reticulatus, Corydoras	56,59
reynoldsi, Corydoras	13
robineae, Corydoras	42,51,52
robustus, Corydoras	44

INDEX
Alphabet

rochai, Aspidoras	9
sanchesi, Corydoras	13
saramaccensis, Corydoras	13
schultzei, Corydoras	104,108
schwartzi, Corydoras	44,45,50
septentrionalis, Corydoras	84
serratus, Corydoras	79
similis, Corydoras	60
simulatus, Corydoras	78
sodalis, Corydoras	57,59
solox, Corydoras	83
sp. "ARAGUAIA", Aspidoras	18
sp. "BAIANINHO II", Corydoras	100
sp. "BRAZIL - LONGNOSE", Corydoras	83
sp. "BRAZIL - SHARPHEAD", Corydoras	52
sp. "FALSO - ROBUSTUS", Corydoras	46
sp. "FRANCISCO", Corydoras	92
sp. "FRANZ: - GUIANA I", Corydoras	81
sp. "GOLD", Corydoras	61
sp. "MOTTLED", Corydoras	83
sp. "PERU - BLACK", Corydoras	100,107
sp. "PERU I", Corydoras	52
sp. "PERU", Corydoras	46
sp. "RIO NEGRO", Corydoras	46
sp. "SAN - JUAN", Corydoras	102,103,104
sp. "THREE - SPOTT - LINES", Corydoras	46
sp. aff. "LONGNOSE" nijsseni, Corydoras	76
sp. aff. aeneus "VENEZUELA", Corydoras	108,109
sp. aff. agassizii, Corydoras	28
sp. aff. amandajaenia, Corydoras	67
sp. aff. ambiacus, Corydoras	31
sp. aff. arcuatus, Corydoras	68
sp. aff. blochi blochi, Corydoras	23
sp. aff. burgessi, Corydoras	71
sp. aff. concolor, Corydoras	110
sp. aff. cortesi, Corydoras	80
sp. aff. crypticus, Corydoras	72
sp. aff. delphax, Corydoras	32
sp. aff. geryi, Corydoras same as C 11	48,52
sp. aff. incolicana, Corydoras	33
sp. aff. multimaculatus, Corydoras	37
sp. aff. nattereri, Corydoras	94
sp. aff. oiapoquensis "PLANE - TAIL", Corydoras	67
sp. aff. ornatus, Corydoras	43
sp. aff. thoracatum, Hoplosternum	120
sp. aff. treitlii, Corydoras	84
sp. aff. vittatus blochi, Corydoras	23
sp. HYBRIDE (panda x oiapoquensis), Corydoras	30
sp. HYBRIDE, Corydoras	72
sp. I, Hoplosternum	120
sp. II, Hoplosternum	121
sp. III, Hoplosternum	121
sp. nijsseni x napoensis HYBRIDE, Corydoras	104
sp. V, Hoplosternum	122
sp. VI, Hoplosternum	121,122
sp."SPOTTED - LINE", Corydoras	46
spilurus, Corydoras	13
splendens, Brochis	20
ssp. intergrade I melanistius, Corydoras	36
ssp. intergrade II melanistius, Corydoras	36
stenocephalus, Corydoras	90
sterbai, Corydoras	53
surinamensis, Corydoras	39,41
sychri, Corydoras	27,34
treitlii "BRAZIL", Corydoras	84
trilineatus, Corydoras	47,56
undulatus, Corydoras	104
urostriata, Dianema	117,118
venezuelanus, Corydoras	104,108
virescens, Corydoras	60
virgulatus, Aspidoras	9
vittatus blochi, Corydoras	21,23
weitzmani, Corydoras	13
wotroi, Corydoras	24,36
xinguensis, Corydoras	61
zygatus, Corydoras	113

ACHTUNG / *ATTENTION*:

Die im alphabetischen Index kursiv gesetzten Artnamen sind Synonyme.

The names written in italic-style in the alphabetical index are synonyms.

Index der Bildautoren
index of the photographers

Dieter Bork

1xS18050, 1xS18135, 1xS18270, 1xS18460, 1xS18690, 1xS18693, 1xS19165, 1xS19265, 1xS19410, 1xS19511, 1xS19512, 1xS19595, 1xS19820, 1xS19932, 1xS20190, 2xS20822

Ernst v. Drachenfels

1xS.81

Hans-Georg Evers

1xS.30, 1xS.34, 1xS.98, 1xS.99, 1xS06102, 1xS06119, 1xS06123, 1xS06140, 1xS06150, 1xS09105, 1xS09110, 1xS18025, 1xS18060, 1xS18070, 1xS18085, 1xS18090, 1xS18100, 1xS18105, 1xS18145, 1xS18150, 1xS18155, 1xS18160, 1xS18230, 1xS18235, 1xS18285, 1xS18295, 1xS18395, 1xS18405, 1xS18415, 1xS18545, 1xS18565, 1xS18567, 1xS18600, 1xS18650, 1xS18665, 1xS18675, 1xS18680, 1xS18691, 1xS18692, 1xS18730, 1xS18765, 1xS18770, 1xS18823, 1xS18870, 1xS18900, 1xS18925, 1xS18945, 1xS18970, 1xS19010, 1xS19022, 1xS19040, 1xS19088, 1xS19098, 1xS19135, 1xS19150, 1xS19175, 1xS19260, 1xS19270, 1xS19270, 1xS19280, 1xS19395, 1xS19410, 1xS19430, 1xS19440, 1xS19450, 1xS19455, 1xS19515, 1xS19565, 1xS19587, 1xS19589, 1xS19600, 1xS19650, 1xS19665, 1xS19680, 1xS19690, 1xS19722, 1xS19775, 1xS19860, 1xS19910, 1xS20000, 1xS20005, 1xS20020, 1xS20040, 1xS20050, 1xS20060, 1xS20070, 1xS20110, 1xS20120, 1xS20160, 1xS20170, 1xS20180, 1xS20200, 1xS20220, 1xS20260, 1xS20330, 1xS20370, 1xS20405, 1xS20406, 1xS20409, 1xS20410, 1xS20411, 1xS20412, 1xS20413, 1xS20416, 1xS20417, 1xS20418, 1xS20419, 1xS20421, 1xS20424, 1xS20428, 1xS20429, 1xS20430, 1xS20438, 1xS20439, 1xS20440, 1xS20441, 1xS20442, 1xS20443, 1xS20444, 1xS20446, 1xS20750, 1xS20770, 1xS20800, 1xS21000, 1xS21050, 2xS06121, 2xS18015, 2xS18326, 2xS18355, 2xS18550, 2xS18600, 2xS18732, 2xS18755, 2xS18815, 2xS18820, 2xS18821, 2xS18853, 2xS19005, 2xS19080, 2xS19105, 2xS19200, 2xS19510, 2xS19555, 2xS19692, 2xS19850, 2xS20403, 2xS20422, 2xS20426, 3xS06145, 3xS18585, 3xS18980, 3xS19120, 3xS19210, 3xS20407, 4xS18160, 4xS18530, 4xS19955, 4xS20030

Dietmar Franz

1xS39048, 2xS39045, 2xS39047, 4xS39046

Dr. Hanns Joachim Franke

1S.64, 1xS.24, 1xS.39, 1xS.42, 1xS.47, 1xS.69, 1xS.70, 1xS18070, 1xS18145, 1xS18270, 1xS18285, 1xS18395, 1xS18565, 1xS18567, 1xS18605, 1xS18640, 1xS18765, 1xS18775, 1xS18810, 1xS18851, 1xS18903, 1xS18945, 1xS18970, 1xS19010, 1xS19020, 1xS19030, 1xS19055, 1xS19095, 1xS19138, 1xS19210, 1xS19260, 1xS19300, 1xS19315, 1xS19340, 1xS19375, 1xS19397, 1xS19430, 1xS19450, 1xS19723, 1xS19755, 1xS19810, 1xS19862, 1xS19970, 1xS20000, 1xS20230, 1xS20401, 1xS20770, 1xS20800, 1xS20802, 1xS20820, 1xS20840, 1xS20900, 1xS21050, 2xS.115, 2xS18025, 2xS18471, 2xS18600, 2xS18800, 2xS19565, 2xS19585, 2xS19765, 2xS19775, 2xS20080

Jürgen Glaser

1xS18205, 1xS18640, 1xS18733, 1xS19265, 1xS19275, 1xS19586, 1xS19860, 1xS19913, 1xS20008, 1xS21050, 2xS19342

Hans J. Mayland

1xS.114, 1xS.98, 1xS06102, 1xS06119, 1xS09105, 1xS09110, 1xS09123, 1xS18025, 1xS18096, 1xS18160, 1xS18210, 1xS18288, 1xS18289, 1xS18295, 1xS18398, 1xS18471, 1xS18530, 1xS18595, 1xS18604, 1xS18605, 1xS18665, 1xS18675, 1xS18790, 1xS18800, 1xS18800, 1xS18810, 1xS19010, 1xS19030, 1xS19040, 1xS19085, 1xS19095, 1xS19175, 1xS19200, 1xS19300, 1xS19315, 1xS19396, 1xS19430, 1xS19450, 1xS19470, 1xS19535, 1xS19588, 1xS19635, 1xS19665, 1xS19690, 1xS19700, 1xS19710, 1xS19724, 1xS19810, 1xS19863, 1xS19866, 1xS19911, 1xS19980, 1xS20003, 1xS20004, 1xS20270, 1xS20402, 1xS20414, 1xS20420, 1xS20432, 1xS20760, 1xS20800, 1xS20900, 1xS20940, 1xS20942, 1xS21003, 1xS21005, 1xS21050, 1xS39040, 1xS39070, 2xS.118, 2xS06110, 2xS18770, 2xS19250, 2xS19251, 2xS19590, 3xS20405

H.J. Mayland/Verlag A.C.S.

1xS18015, 1xS18095, 1xS18110, 1xS18295, 1xS18320, 1xS18325, 1xS18419, 1xS18567, 1xS18590, 1xS18652, 1xS18980, 1xS19055, 1xS19281, 1xS19340, 1xS19514, 1xS19630, 1xS19670, 1xS19850, 1xS19914, 2xS18375

Burkhard Migge/Hans Rheinhard

1xS.21, 1xS18050, 1xS18060, 1xS18298, 1xS18355, 1xS19586, 1xS19755, 1xS19765, 1xS19915, 2xS39071

Hans J. Richter / Verlag A.C.S.

1xS18080, 1xS18160, 1xS18320, 1xS18825, 1xS18850, 1xS18852, 1xS19040, 1xS19150, 1xS19430, 1xS20840, 1xS20900, 2xS18470, 2xS39070

Friedrich und Dietrich Rössel

1xS18050, 1xS18245, 1xS18270, 1xS18365, 1xS18455, 1xS18602, 1xS18906, 1xS19190, 1xS19470, 1xS19860, 1xS19935, 1xS20150, 1xS20320, 1xS20380, 1xS20408, 1xS20445, 1xS39020, 2xS18575, 2xS19452

Index der Bildautoren
index of the photographers

Erwin Schraml

1xS06121, 1xS06123, 1xS09110, 1xS18035, 1xS18040, 1xS18041, 1xS18045, 1xS18065, 1xS18095, 1xS18200, 1xS18290, 1xS18295, 1xS18320, 1xS18405, 1xS18515, 1xS18565, 1xS18585, 1xS18595, 1xS18600, 1xS18615, 1xS18675, 1xS18745, 1xS18746, 1xS18747, 1xS18770, 1xS18870, 1xS18906, 1xS19010, 1xS19086, 1xS19099, 1xS19175, 1xS19370, 1xS19398, 1xS19410, 1xS19433, 1xS19455, 1xS19530, 1xS19537, 1xS19587, 1xS19650, 1xS19690, 1xS19700, 1xS19767, 1xS19778, 1xS19820, 1xS19840, 1xS19867, 1xS19868, 1xS19932, 1xS19980, 1xS19983, 1xS20000, 1xS20431, 1xS20825, 1xS20845, 1xS20950, 2xS09120, 2xS19020, 2xS19454, 2xS20405, 2xS20770, 3xS18822, 3xS20434

Ingo Seidel

1xS.25, 1xS.50, 1xS.50, 1xS.54, 1xS.65, 1xS.81, 1xS.91, 1xS09125, 1xS11105, 1xS18035, 1xS18320, 1xS18418, 1xS18530, 1xS18585, 1xS18600, 1xS18650, 1xS18730, 1xS18790, 1xS18824, 1xS19030, 1xS19080, 1xS19120, 1xS19155, 1xS19175, 1xS19190, 1xS19270, 1xS19440, 1xS19450, 1xS19513, 1xS19589, 1xS19690, 1xS19695, 1xS19722, 1xS19765, 1xS19810, 1xS19820, 1xS19865, 1xS19910, 1xS19912, 1xS19916, 1xS19980, 1xS20220, 1xS20250, 1xS20290, 1xS20300, 1xS20310, 1xS20360, 1xS20403, 1xS20409, 1xS20416, 1xS20419, 1xS20424, 1xS20425, 1xS20429, 1xS20735, 1xS20940, 1xS21000, 1xS39041, 1xS39048, 1xS39049, 1xS39050, 2xS.59, 2xS18675, 2xS20090, 2xS20405, 7xS20750

Frank Warzel

1xS19722

Uwe Werner

1xS06126, 1xS11108, 1xS20090, 1xS39025, 1xS39030, 1xS39070

Erwin Schraml/Verlag A.C.S.

1xS.107, 1xS18200, 1xS18555, 1xS18775, 1xS18960, 1xS19000, 1xS19155, 1xS19160, 1xS19200, 1xS19280, 1xS19588, 1xS19668, 1xS19670, 1xS19710, 1xS19766, 1xS19850, 1xS19935, 1xS19953, 1xS19970, 1xS20270, 1xS20340, 1xS20421, 1xS20433, 1xS21004, 1xS31130, 1xS31135, 2xS06115, 2xS18455, 2xS18555, 2xS20415

Ingo Seidel/Verlag A.C.S.

1xS18850, 1xS18925

Literaturhinweise
literature tips

Dr. Burgess, Warren E. (1989)
Atlas of Catfishes
T.F.H. Publications, Inc. Neptune City

Evers, Hans-Georg (1994)
Panzerwelse
Verlag Eugen Ulmer Stuttgart (Hohenheim)

Franke, Hans-Joachim (1985)
Handbuch der Welskunde
Landbuch Verlag Hannover

Kobayagawa, Midori (1991)
Faszination Welse
Bede Verlag Kollnburg

Seuß, Werner (1993)
Corydoras
Dähne Verlag Ettlingen

Quellennachweis
list of sources

Cope, E.D. (1872): On the fishes of the Ambyiacua River. Proc. Acad. Nat. Sci., 23: 250-294 + pl.

Fowler, H.W. (1941): Los Peces del Peru Catalogo sistematico de los peces que habitan en aguas peruanes (Continuacion). Bol. Mus. Hist. Nat. >Javier Prado< 5 (16): 466-487.

Fowler, H.: (1915): Notes on nematognathous fishes. Proc. Acad. nat. Sci. Philadelphia, 67: 203 - 243.

Geisler, R. (1996): Corydoras baderi, ein neuer Panzerwels und sein Lebensraum im Grenzgebiet Brasilien-Surinam Senck. biol., 50 (5-6) : 353-357.

Luckow, Rolf: Artenliste Panzerwelse in Kooperation mit H.-G. Evers

Nijssen, H. (1970): Revision of the Surinam catfishes of the genus Corydoras Lacepede, 1803 (Pisces, Siluriformes, Callichthydae). Beaufortia, 19 (250): 89-98.
- (1971): Two new species and one new subspecies of the South American catfish genus Corydoras (Pisces, Siluriformes, Callichthyidae). Beaufortia, 19 (250): 89-98.
- (1972): Records of the catfish genus Corydoras from Brazil and French Guiana with descriptions of eight new species (Pisces, Siluriformes, Callichthydiae). Neth. Journal Zool., 21 (4): 412-433.

Nijssen, H. and I.H.J. Isbrücker (1967): Notes on the Guiana species of Corydoras Lacepede, 1803, with descriptions of seven new species and designation of a neotype for Corydoras punctatus (Bloch, 1794) - (pisces, Cypriniformes, Callichthydae). Zool. Meded. Leiden, 42 (5): 21-49.
- (1970): The South American catfish genus Brochis Cope, 1872 (Pisces, Siluriformes, Callichthydae). Beaufortia 18 (236): 151-168.

Quellenverzeichnis
list of sources

- (1976a): The South American plated catfish genus Aspidoras R. v. Ihering, 1907, with description of nine new species from Brazil (Pisces, Siluriformes, Callichthydae). Bijdr. t. d. Dierk., 46 (1): 107-131.
- (1976b): Corydoras ornatus, a new species of callichthyid catfish from the Rio Tapajos drainage, Brazil (Pisces, Siluriformes, Callichthyidae). Bul. Zool. Mus. Univ. Amsterdam, 5 (15): 125-129.
- (1980): Aspidoras virgulatus n. sp., a plated catfish from Espirito Santo, Brazil. Bul. Zool. Mus. Univ. Amsterdam, 7 (13): 133-138.
- (1982): Corydoras boehlkei, a new catfish from the Rio Caura System in Venezuela. Proc. Acad. Nat. Sci. Phil., 134: 139-142.

- (1983a): Review of the genus Corydoras from Colombia, with descriptions of two new species (Pisces, Siluriformes, Callichthyidae). Beaufortia, 33 (5): 53-71.
- (1983b): Review of the genus Corydoras from Colombia, with descriptions of two new species (Pisces, Siluriformes, Callichthyidae). Beaufortia, 33 (5): 53-71.
- (1983c): Sept especes nouvelles de Poissons-Chats cuirasses de genre Corydoras Lacspede, 1803, de Guyane francaise, de Bolivie, d`Argentine, du Surinam et du Brazil. Rev. fr. Aquariol. 12 (1): 65-76.
- (1986): Cinq especes nouvelles des Poissons-Chats cuirasses de genre Corydoras Lacèpède, 1803, du Perou et del`Equateur. Rev. fr. Aquariol. 12 (1): 65-76.

Weitzmann, S.H. and G.S. Myers (1960): New Colombian Fishes: Corydoras reynoldsi - new species. Stanf. Ichth. Bull., 7 (4): 105-109.

Weitzmann, S.H. and H. Nijssen (1970): Four new species and one new subspecies of the catfish genus Corydoras from Ecuador, Colombia and Brazil. Beaufortia, 18 (233): 119-132.